WITH LOVE AND IRONY

BOOKS BY LIN YUTANG
Published by THE JOHN DAY COMPANY

MY COUNTRY AND MY PEOPLE

THE IMPORTANCE OF LIVING

MOMENT IN PEKING

WITH LOVE AND IRONY

LIN YUTANG

WITH LOVE AND IRONY

Illustrated by Kurt Wiese

BLUE RIBBON BOOKS

Garden City, New York

PR
9470.9
L5
W53
1945

BLUE RIBBON BOOKS Reprint Edition, 1945, by special
arrangement with THE JOHN DAY COMPANY

PRINTED IN THE UNITED STATES OF AMERICA

TO THE MEMORY OF

HEYWOOD BROUN

FRIEND OF MEN

ACKNOWLEDGMENT

The author wishes to acknowledge the kindness of the editors of *Asia, Cosmopolitan, The Forum,* and the *New York Times* for permission to reprint several chapters in this volume which originally appeared in those periodicals.

CONTENTS

vii

INTRODUCTION

WHEN I was living in Nanking, China, I followed with sharp interest several new and struggling little magazines, because of my concern with what was taking place around me in a revolutionary China. There was one in English called *The China Critic*. I read it from cover to cover every week, since in it young Chinese intellectuals were expressing their thoughts and hopes. Their language was English, partly because they wanted English-speaking readers, partly because they wrote, some of them, more easily in English than in Chinese. Then there began to appear in its pages a column entitled "The Little Critic," signed by one Lin Yutang, of whom until then I had never heard. The column was unvaryingly a fresh, keen, accurate comment on some aspect or occurrence of daily life, political or social. What won my first admiration was its fearlessness. At a time when it was really dangerous to criticize those in power, The Little Critic criticized boldly and freely, saving himself, I am sure, only by the humor and wit with which his opinions were expressed. This wit, clothing fearlessness where others were timid, mercilessness where no mercy was due, and sympathy for and appreciation of the common people of China, bourgeoisie as well as proletariat, soon drew the attention of many readers besides myself, and people began to ask, "Who is this Lin Yutang?"

Many readers in many countries have asked that since,

and have found out who he is. His books explain him. But this book explains him in a peculiar way. It contains the kind of writing which is perhaps above all others most native to Lin Yutang's genius, and genius unquestionably he is. These writings represent the sparkling, thrusting quality of his thought. They are the instinctive expression of the working of his mind, glancing, darting, penetrating, laughing.

Over a period of years Lin Yutang has written down these short pungent pieces, and from them, past and present, this book has been made. They are not all here, by any means, for many of them were timely and are no longer in point. But enough are here to show variety, and variety is Lin Yutang's delight, although his interest can hold a subject long and deeply, too, when it is profound.

There is another thing I might tell. One night in 1933 I was dining in Lin Yutang's home, then in Shanghai. We had been speaking of foreign writers about China, when he said suddenly, "I should like to write a book telling exactly how I feel about China."

"You are the one who could do it," I replied with utmost enthusiasm. I had longed for just such a book from a Chinese. Lin Yutang wrote it, and it was called *My Country and My People*. The basic sources of that book, and indeed many passages in it and in *The Importance of Living* which followed it, were first in the columns of "The Little Critic." Before either was written, I gathered together some of those columns and sent them to America, to *Asia Magazine*. One of them was published in that magazine, and was the first work of Lin Yutang to appear in this country. It was "The Lost Mandarin," which is included in the present volume.

Lin Yutang has spent the last months in the heart of China.

He has shared with millions of others the cruel experiences of war. But whatever those experiences have been he will remain what he is in this book, the little critic, humorous, wise, and unaffected in his sincerity.

PEARL S. BUCK

WITH LOVE AND IRONY

WITH LOVE AND IRONY

1

THE ENGLISH AND THE CHINESE

ONE is often tempted nowadays to reflect on the white man, because the spectacle of present-day Europe is extremely thought-provoking.

We cannot help asking why Europe is in such a mess, because where human events are in a mess, the human beings must be at fault. We are forced to ask ourselves, "What are the psychological limitations of the European which make peace so difficult in Europe?" What are the peculiarities of the European's mental make-up? And, by mental make-up, I do not mean intelligence or thinking pure and simple but all the psychological reactions to things.

I should never for a moment question the intelligence of the European race. But the sad part of it is that, after all, intelligence has very little to do with the course of human events, which are mostly dictated by our animal passions.

Human history is not the product of the wise direction of human reason, but is shaped by the forces of emotion—our dreams, our pride, our greed, our fears, and our desire for revenge. Europe is still dominated not by intelligence but by the animal passions of fear and revenge. Progress in Europe is the result not of the white man's thinking but of his lack of thinking. If there were a single supreme Human Intelligence today put at the head of Europe and guiding her entire destiny, Europe would not be what she is. Modern Europe is being ruled not by a single supreme Human Intelligence but by three men with big and powerful jaws— Signor Mussolini, Adolf Hitler, and Josef Stalin.

This is not a mere accident. Some faces are like triangles, with the broad base situated below (the dictators and men of action), and some faces are like inverted triangles (the men of intelligence and thinkers, Bertrand Russell, for example). The men of intelligence and the men of action belong to two entirely different types. The German nation can swear allegiance to "God and Hitler," but, if an English Nazi party were to swear allegiance to "God and Bertrand Russell," Bertrand Russell would die of shame. So long as Europe is ruled by these men with big and powerful jaws and so long as she is willing to be ruled by men with big and powerful jaws, Europe must continue along her present lines of development and head for the abyss she is heading for today.

Every nation dreams, and acts more or less completely on her dreams. Human history is the result of the conflict of our ideals and realities, and the adjustment between ideals and reality determines the peculiar development of that nation. The U.S.S.R. is the result of the Russian capacity for dreaming; the French Republic was the result of the French passion for abstract ideas; the British Empire is the result of the wonderfully robust common sense of the English and their utter freedom from logical reasoning; and the German Nazi regime is the result of the German love for a common front and mass action.

I write of the English character because I think I understand England better than these other countries. I feel that the spirit of the English people is more akin to the spirit of the Chinese people, for both nations are worshipers of realism and common sense. There are many points of similarity between the English and the Chinese in their modes of thinking and even in their modes of speech. Both peoples have a profound distrust of logic and are extremely suspicious of arguments that are too perfect. We believe that when an argument is too logical it cannot be true. And both countries are gifted more at doing the right things than at giving happy reasons for doing them. All Englishmen love a good liar, and so do the Chinese. We love to call a thing by anything except its right name. Of course there are many points of dissimilarity (the Chinese are more emotional, for instance), and the Chinese and English sometimes exasperate each other; but I am digging at the roots of our racial make-up.

Let us analyze the strength of the English character and see how England's glorious career as a nation arises from it. We all know that England has had not only a glorious career but also a positively amazing career. England always had the knack of doing the right thing and calling it by the wrong name, as today, for instance, she calls the English democracy a monarchy. For this reason, it is very difficult to appreciate the quality of English greatness. The English nation has been misunderstood, and it takes a Chinese to understand the English racial character properly. The English people have been accused of hypocrisy, inconsistency, a genius for "muddling through," and a notorious lack of logic. I am making a defense of English inconsistency and English common sense. The accusation of hypocrisy is unjust and arises from a lack of true understanding and appreciation of the English character. I think, as a Chinese, I can understand the English character better than Englishmen understand themselves.

I am trying here chiefly to give a point of view for a true appreciation of England's greatness. In order to appreciate England one has to have a certain contempt for logic. All this misunderstanding of the English people arises from a perverted idea of the true function of thinking. There is always a danger that we regard abstract thinking as the highest function of the human mind, to be valued over and above simple common sense. Now the first function of nations, as of animals, is to know how to live, and, unless you learn how to live and adjust yourself to changing circumstances, all your thinking is futile and a perversion of the normal function of the human brain.

We all have the perverted idea that the human brain is an organ for thinking. Nothing is further from the truth. That view, I submit, is biologically incorrect and unsound. Lord Balfour has wisely said that "the human brain is as much an organ for seeking food as the pig's snout." After all, the human brain is only an enlarged piece of the spinal column whose first function is to sense danger and preserve life. We were animals before we became thinkers. This so-called logical reasoning is only a very much belated development in the animal world, and even now it is still highly imperfect.

Man is only a half-thinking and half-feeling animal. The type of thinking which helps one to get food and get along in life is a higher, not a lower, type of thinking, because this kind of thinking is always sounder. This type of thinking is usually called common sense.

Now action without thinking may be foolish, but action without common sense is always disastrous. A nation with a robust common sense is not a nation that does no thinking but rather a nation which has subjugated its thinking to its instinct for life and made them harmonious. Thinking of this type profits from the instinct for life but is never against it. Too much thinking will bring about mankind's destruction.

The English people think, too, but never allow themselves to be lost in their own thoughts and logical abstractions. That is the greatness of the English mind and the reason for England's ability always to do the right thing at the right moment. It is also the reason for the English ability to fight the right war on the right side. She has always fought the right war and always given wrong reasons for her choice. That is the reason for England's amazing power and vitality. You may call it "muddling through" and inconsistency and hypocrisy. At the bottom of it all is the robust English common sense and a level-headed instinct for life.

In other words, the first law of nations as of individuals is the law of self-preservation, and, the more a nation is able to adjust itself to changing circumstances, the sounder is her instinct for life, logic or no logic. "Consistency," Cicero says, "is the virtue of small minds." The English capacity for inconsistency is merely a sign of England's greatness.

Take the amazing British Empire, for example, today still

the greatest empire in the world. How did the English people build it? By an entire absence of logical reasoning. The
greatness of the British Empire is based, you may say, on
English sportsmanship, English endurance, English guts,
and the incorruptibility of English judges. All that is true,
but there is a greater reason: the greatness of the British Empire is based on the English lack of cerebration. The lack
of cerebration, or insufficient cerebration, produces moral
strength. The British Empire exists because the Englishman
is so cocksure of himself and his own superiority.

No nation can go about conquering the world unless she
is quite certain of her "civilizing" mission. The moment,
however, that you begin to think and see something in the
other nation or the other fellow and his ways, your moral
conviction leaves you, and your empire collapses. The British
Empire still stands today because the Englishman still believes that his ways are the only correct ways and because
he cannot tolerate anybody who does not conform to his
standards.

Thus the British Empire itself is based on an entirely illogical proposition. Its foundations actually date back to the
pirate days of the supreme struggle with the Spanish Empire,
in the time of Queen Elizabeth. But, when pirates were necessary for the expansion of the British Empire, England was
able to produce enough pirates to meet the situation, and she
glorified her pirates. Later, when the industrial revolution
called for colonial markets, she developed an instinct for
founding colonies and made another astounding discovery
of her civilizing influence. Soon an English poet, Rudyard
Kipling, discovered the white man's burden, and the consciousness of the white man's burden and England's civilizing influence helped Englishmen to carry on as nothing else

could. Of course nothing could be more ridiculous than all this, but nothing showed a sounder instinct for life.

Yet, if you think that this is mere thick-headedness and there is nothing more to it than a merely negative virtue, consider the other side of the picture. Certainly the development of the British Empire is unprecedented in mankind's history, and certainly such an empire can not be held together merely by an absence of logic. In the hands of any other nation, the British Empire would have fallen by its own weight, for the problem of holding together an empire from Australia to Canada must tax the most statesmanlike mind. Only the English mind could have solved it, and it did so by inventing the British Commonwealth. The British Commonwealth is actually a league of nations, with the difference that it is a league of nations which really works. The English people are probably unaware that it is a league of nations, for they have the knack of doing a thing without knowing what it is. I don't know how the English people discovered the formula, but somehow or other they have discovered it or stumbled into it by their sheer common sense and the capacity for adjustment to realities.

Or take the case of the English language. The English language is today the nearest equivalent to an international language. How did the English people do it? By an equally absurd absence of logic, by the sheer stubbornness of the Englishman in refusing to speak anybody else's language. A Chinese speaks English when he is in England, speaks French when he is in France, and speaks German when he is in Germany. But an Englishman speaks only English everywhere. The English maxim is:

> When you are traveling in Rome,
> Do exactly as at home.

This is the only poem I ever composed in English.

It is the most illogical thing but again it has turned out to be the right thing, and English today has established itself as incontrovertibly *the* international language.

And so on in all the different aspects of her national life. Her Anglican Church is a theological anomaly. Theologically, it is a hodgepodge of Roman mutton with English sauce, a popish theology without a pope, being merely the expression of the political sense of Henry VIII and Queen Elizabeth. It is absurd, it is ridiculously illogical, and today it is hopelessly antiquated, but a few years ago the English Parliament still refused to revise its prayer book. It is a supreme example of the English spirit of compromise. But it is a church that works and survives to this day.

The English constitution is another masterpiece of English patchwork, and yet in spite of its being a patchwork it offers the English people a real guarantee of their civil rights.

England's great universities offer another instance of a strange conglomeration of colleges without rhyme or reason. Oxford has thirty colleges, and no one can tell you the reason why there must be thirty and not twenty-nine, and yet Oxford remains among the world's truest seats of learning.

The English form of government is in itself a contradiction, a monarchy in name and a democracy in reality, but somehow the English people do not feel any conflict in it. The English profess the greatest love for and loyalty to their king and then proceed to limit the expenditures of the royal household through their Parliament. Some day England will yet become a bolshevik state, with the English king still on his throne and under the leadership of a most die-hard conservative cabinet. England is already a socialist state today, taxing her aristocracy out of their landed estates and castles

—without calling it by the name of socialism—and England may in a short time turn Laborite, but one feels the process will take place so smoothly that there will be no violent shake-up. I feel confident that the basis of English democracy will stand the strain.

And so there goes the Englishman with his umbrella (and unashamed of his umbrella), refusing to talk any language but his own, demanding marmalade in an African jungle and unable to forgive his "boy" for not producing holly and a plum pudding in an African desert on Christmas eve, so sure of himself, so terribly cocksure of himself, and so terribly decent. There is an inevitability about his words and actions and gestures when he is not looking like a dumb, persecuted animal. You can predict exactly what an Englishman will do even when he sneezes. He will take out his handkerchief—for he always has a handkerchief—and mutter something about the beastly cold. And you can tell what is going on in his mind about Bovril and going home to have a hot foot bath, all as inevitable as that the sun is going to rise in the east the next morning. But you cannot upset him. That cheekiness is not very lovely, but it is very imposing. In fact, he has conquered the world with that bluff and that cheekiness; and his success in doing so is his best justification.

For myself, I am rather taken by that cheekiness, the cheekiness of a man who thinks that any country is God-forsaken whose people do not take Bovril and do not produce the inevitable white handkerchief when the correct moment comes. One is lured to look behind that extremely brazen front and take a peep at his inner soul. For the Englishman is imposing, just as solitude is imposing. A man who can sit all by himself at a club party and look damned comfortable is always imposing.

Of course there is something in it. His soul is not such bad stuff, and his cheekiness is not just side and airs. I sometimes feel that the Bank of England can never fail, just because the English people believe so, that it cannot be closed simply because it isn't being done. The Bank of England is decent. So is the English Post Office. So is the Manufacturers' Life Assurance. So is the whole British Empire, all so decent, so inevitably decent. I am sure Confucius himself would have found England the ideal country to live in. He would be pleased with the London "bobby" assisting old women across the street and he would be pleased to see children and minors addressing their elders with their "Yes, sir's."

China, too, was a land that was terribly decent and terribly cocksure of herself. The Chinese people, too, were a people full of common sense and glorifying their common sense at the expense of logic. If there was anything the Chinese were incapable of, it was scientific reasoning, which was totally absent from their literature. The Chinese mind thinks by leaps and starts, and it often arrives at the same truth but by a quicker way, by sheer intuition. The Chinese mind had a knack of leaving out the unessentials and keeping a tight hold of the essentials of life. It had, above all, common sense and a wisdom of life; and it had humor and it could face a logical inconsistency with a clear conscience and great complacency.

Much of that wisdom and humor is now lost, and that good sense which distinguished our ancient life is now decayed. The modern Chinese is a freakish, peevish, and neurasthenic individual, having lost his equitable temper through the loss of self-confidence brought about by the misfortunes of China's national life in the last century and the humiliations of having to adjust herself to a new way of life.

But ancient China had common sense and a large measure of it. The most typical of Chinese thinkers was Confucius, and the most typical of English thinkers was Dr. Johnson, both philosophers of common sense. If Confucius and Dr. Johnson had met, they would have smiled and understood each other perfectly. Both could not suffer fools gladly and both would put up with no nonsense. Both showed penetrating wisdom and a firm judgment. Both used the same rule-of-thumb method and both worked on a patchwork of ideas. And both had utter contempt for mere consistency. Mencius said of Confucius that he was the saint of opportunists, and Confucius twice said of himself that with him "*yes* can do and *no* also can do."

And the strange thing was that the Chinese worshiped this great master because he *was* a saint of opportunists—which was no term of opprobium in Chinese—because he understood life too profoundly to be merely consistent. Outwardly there was nothing to admire in this village schoolmaster. But the Chinese worshiped him rather than the more brilliant Chuangtze or the more logical Shang Yang or the more thoroughgoing Wang Anshih. There was nothing striking about Confucius except his love of the commonplace and nothing extraordinary about him except his platitudes. The only thing divine about him was his great humanity. As Dr. John C. H. Wu puts it: "He was too moral to be moralistic, too pure to be puritanical, too broadly human to be all-too-human, too consistently moderate to be immoderate even in the virtue of moderation."

There could not have been a more uninteresting character. It takes a Chinese people to worship such a man, as it took an English people to worship Ramsay MacDonald, whose political life was a supreme effort to be inconsistent in the English manner, which is the grand manner. A Laborite, MacDonald one day went up the steps of Number 10 Down-ing Street, sniffed its air, and felt happy. The world, he felt, was quite likable and secure and he proceeded to do his best to make it more secure. Having come to such a stage, he had no more scruples about committing his Laborite prin-ciples to the winds than Confucius would have. For Con-fucius would have approved of Ramsay MacDonald as he would have approved of Dr. Johnson. Thus do the great spirits meet across the ages.

What Europe needs today and what the modern world needs is not more intellectual brilliance but more life wis-dom. The English have no logic but have wisdom in the Chinese sense. One feels somehow that European life has been more secure and the course of Europe's historical de-velopment more steady for England's presence. There are so few things one can be sure about that it does one good to see a man who can be so sure of himself.

The great difference between England and China is that there is more manliness in the English culture and more feminine cunning in the Chinese culture. China would do well to learn a little manliness from England, and England would do well to learn more moderation and mellow under-standing of life and the art of living from the Chinese. The true test of a civilization is not how you are able to conquer and to kill but how you can get the greatest kick out of life; and for these humble arts of peace, like feeding birds and raising orchids and cooking mushrooms and being happy in simple surroundings, the West has still a lot to learn from China.

Someone has said that the ideal life is to live in an English country home, engage a Chinese cook, marry a Japanese wife, and take a French mistress. If we could all do that, we should have moved on in the arts of peace and could then afford to forget the arts of war. We would then know how to live, and forget how to kill. Christians may object to this scheme, but I believe such co-operation in the art of living will mark a new era of international understanding and good will and make the modern world safer to live in.

2

THE AMERICANS

IN CHINA, one hears tales about America and the Americans. On the whole, they are much like the tales one hears in France or England. America is a country where men eat hot dogs, women chew gum, and children lick ice-cream cones. The idea conveyed, however, is not that *some* Americans do these things, but that every man eats hot dogs, every woman moves her jaws perpetually up and down, and every child holds an ice-cream cone in his hand.

"Isn't that a curious world?" we remark among our-selves. And then we hear about one-hundred-two-story skyscrapers, motor cars going about underground like earth-worms, railroads dashing in mid-air, restaurants where you put in a nickel and a roast chicken springs auto-matically upon your table, staircases where you go up without lifting a leg, policemen all six feet tall, women going about with hardly a thing on, et cetera. Unbeliev-able but true, since many of us are able to see all this with our own eyes on the movie screen. Oh, America!

Worse than that, we hear that in America everybody is punctual: that when an American makes an appointment for nine o'clock, he invariably turns up at nine o'clock; that everybody is dashing about the streets and nobody wastes a single minute; and that the whole pattern of life is organized like a fire department and every individual is like a railroad, running on schedule. We hear that every-body in Hollywood is terribly rich and contented and happy; that everybody is a Christian in America, and that the Daughters of the American Revolution are the great guard-ians of American democracy; that Negroes are being lynched every day, and gangsters are lying round every street corner in Chicago; that in this land of Liberty everybody is dancing and "making whoopee"; and that in this land of Equality, everybody can pat everybody else on the shoulder. . . .

So it was with wondering eyes that I came and *observed* America, but being a sensible man, I expected neither too much nor too little. That was my salvation. Scientifically, I believed everything possible, and humanly, I believed many things were impossible. In everything pertaining to science, I found the facts had not been exaggerated; but in everything pertaining to human behavior, I was confirmed in my belief that Americans are not very different from the Chinese.

I was prepared for the worst and the best. Happy was I when I found myself justified in expecting American women still to look after their husbands' stomachs like Chinese women, although they had never heard of Confucius.

I went into an American drugstore and began there to read American humanity. An American drugstore is perfect for this purpose. It has four C's; Cigars for men, Chocolates for women, Candies for children, and Cough Drops for old people. I found men buying cigars, women buying chocolates, children buying candies, and old people buying cough drops. And I found the women and children perhaps happier than the men and the old people, but certainly happier than the women and the children of other countries.

For America is the land of women and children. It is called the New World, while Europe and Asia are called the Old World. When you speak of the New World, you mean simply that the American women are new and the American children are new—are quite unlike the women and children of Asia and Europe. The women and children are what make America a new world.

In America woman is being given a break. Giving a woman a break always scared an Old World male, especially an Asiatic. "What would happen?" is the instinctive question of the protective male. What would happen if you gave woman a break; for instance, if you let a young girl loose in the wide, wide world?

I was a little shocked to find that after woman was given such a break, *nothing happened*. Apparently, she could take care of herself. I began to wonder: Why did we males in the Old World ever bother to take care of women at all?

After long hours of philosophizing, I am now willing to make the brave and hard admission that women are just human beings like men—equal in ability to make judgments and mistakes, if you give them the same world experience and contacts; in ability to do efficient work and keep a cool head, if you give them the same business training; in social outlook, if you don't shut them up in the home; and finally, in the capacity to rule and misrule, for if women should rule the world, they couldn't possibly make a greater mess of it than men have in present-day Europe.

I had been led by readings of earlier feminists to believe that the emancipated women didn't want to marry, and I find that women on the whole are too smart for that sort of nonsense. If many of them don't marry, it isn't because they don't know what is good. They have too much common sense for that. No woman can live without the love of a man and still be a happy biological animal.

There are the American girls, especially the brilliant ones, who have been cheated, cheated out of their right of marriage, cheated out of their right to capture a man by all the available wiles, traps, and tricks at their sex's command, cheated, I say, by a biologically unsound philosophy. Whatever you say about the suppression of woman in China, remember that every Chinese woman gets married. That simply means there is a man in this world over whose destiny, by the grace of God and the invention of society, she rules. There is at least one man in flesh and blood a Chinese woman can subject, however high and mighty the male sex as a whole has subjected her—one man whom God has placed in her hands to continue His work of molding and making him. We Chinese have a famous saying that man is made of clay and woman of water, meaning that is why man is so dirty and heavy and woman so light and pure, and the water permeates and molds the clay. I am sure the whole Genesis story of man's creation has to be written over again with a Chinese touch: Adam was clay and Eve was water, and God merely made a rough unfinished molding of Adam, and told Eve to finish the rest. Every woman who marries a man is but continuing God's work, starting where God or his mother left him. Now the clever American girls think that is beneath their dignity. God does not like them and therefore punishes them with neurasthenia and with loneliness. The earlier the American girls decide they are not going to live alone and like it, the sooner is their salvation. Let them go out of their superfine mansion of philosophy and independence, let them mix their pure water with humble clay, let them combine *yin* with *yang,* and let them face the obvious truth that man and woman reach their full expression, and therefore find their true happiness, only in the harmonious complementing of the other sex—let them do that and see what happens and rediscover an old truth that Old World women discovered long ago.

My only message to American womanhood is a platitude; Go out and get a man, by hook or by crook. The subconscious has already been done to death—let's get back to a simple conscious truth. Go out, get a man, and rear babies, raise chickens and carrots.

We now come to the rock of American democracy, the common man. America is a highly romantic type of democracy, colored by the position of woman and of the common man. The position of woman colors, and is colored by its romanticism, which is the romanticism of Madame de Staël, expansive, humanitarian, cosmopolitan, and emotional. The position of the common man, on the other hand, colors, and is colored by, its democracy.

To understand the position of the common man, it is first necessary to understand the nature of American democracy. American democracy is ultimately based on the ideal of *the greatest goods to the greatest number*, and that is where the common man, representing the greatest number, comes in.

I may be wrong, but I believe that in America it is as an ideal of the "greatest goods," rather than of the intangible "greatest good" merely, that democracy will be appreciated by the people. For only in America does one hear that one can "sell an idea," and that a radio sponsor can "buy an artist."

The common man is the rock of American democracy because he, rather than the gentleman, represents the greatest number, to whom the greatest numbers of things are to be sold, and for whom radio programs and movies are being made—and what is American democracy if the manufacturers don't sell products by the hundreds of thousands and make movies for the millions?

That being so, it is in American democracy that we have life and have it abundantly, for we have motor cars abundantly and magazines abundantly and radio sets abundantly. And so the common man prospers and is having a swell time, and the more common he is, the sweller he becomes.

For only in America have the common men, the women, and the children a chance to discover themselves and their potentialities. Being hospitable to everything new, you put everything in the great pot that is American democracy—

new women, new children, new cures, new fads, new dresses, new games, new schools, new machines, new sofa beds, new jazz—and churn and stew them together. Being of an experimental turn of mind, I am dying to know what will come out of that pot after, say, another fifty years.

3

WHAT I LIKE ABOUT AMERICA

ONE might just as well put it down on paper, once and for all. That will at least provide a ready answer for every question that might be asked of a foreign writer.

Perhaps these likes and dislikes may be all wrong. Perhaps after a longer stay, one will revise one's opinions or even begin to like what one disliked and dislike what one used to like. Of so much less value will those maturer judgments be, to my way of thinking. It will be impossible to recapture those first thrills of new impacts, those first impressions, sensations, bewilderments, and novel surprises. I do not need psychologists to tell me about the law of habit—that the human mind is apt to disregard the discordant, once it has become familiar, and eventually regard everything as reasonable because it is customary.

Also, I do not justify my likes and dislikes. Personal likes and dislikes are things that you do not have to give reasons for. They are just personal likes and dislikes. I like certain things because I like them. To every question about the reason for my preferences, the answer is, "Just because."

Well, then, what do I like about America and what do I dislike? (I am merely trying to put into practice the American principle of free speech.)

I like best of all, in New York, the granite rocks in Central Park, as beautiful in their rugged rhythm as any to be found on high mountaintops; next the squirrels with such beautiful clean fur; and third, the men and women who are able to share with me the delight in those little squirrels. None there are, I suspect, who share with me the delight in the rocks— those silent, immutable rocks.

I like hot dogs but do not like the company I generally find myself in when eating them. I like best of all a glass of tomato juice but hate to drink tomato juice surrounded by bottles of Bromo-Seltzer, packages of Ex-Lax, boxes of aspirin, and a mountain of bath salts, sponges, Schick injectors, electric toasters, toothbrushes, dental creams, kissproof lipsticks, and shaving brushes.

I like to eat raw celery and honeydew melon in the paneled cellar of Louis and Armand or have a bite before the open stands of Nedick's. Either the one or the other, but no soda lunches, if I can help it. There, perched on those rotating disks, I am neither a sophisticated gourmet attending to his food with a religious fervor nor a glorious, carefree tramp, but just a New York hustler, with not enough elbow room in God's universe to pull out a handkerchief comfortably. And if I should yawn and stretch, as every gentleman should after a good meal, I should fall overboard.

I like everything about the radio except its programs. I marvel at the unprecedented opportunity for bringing good music and artistic enjoyment to the home and equally at the proportionately unprecedented absence of good music and artistic enjoyment. I bow in profound admiration before the mysterious wires, coils, switches, and vacuum tubes and the mechanic with wires, coils, and sundry apparatus to catch music from the air; but I tower with supreme contempt over the music finally caught by the mysterious coils, wires, and vacuum tubes. Americans have bad music but good music catchers.

I marvel exceedingly at the complete success with which the rich store of European music is held in abeyance and hidden in shame. Equally do I delight in the announcements of sales, which are the best parts of the programs, because they are the only parts that are sincere.

I love the luscious Burbank pears and fragrant American apples and the rich, resonant voices of Americans and all that is vital and rich and whole. And I hate diluted clam broth and effeminate melodies and robust American college boys crooning pseudosentiments in pseudosoft voices, inevitably rhyming "you" with "blue," and all that is affected, patterned, manufactured, and made to order.

I love the gorgeous American chrysanthemums, as admiration-compelling as any in China, and the unbelievable varieties of orchids in Fifth Avenue flower shops; but I detest the way most of the bouquets are arranged, without any rhythmic vitality or subtle contrast.

I love the ringing laughter of children playing in the park, unafraid of dirt, and the sweet piping of young ladies calling to squirrels. I like seeing pure-faced young mothers with their perambulators and single ladies sprawling on the ground taking naps, their faces barely covered by newspapers, and all that speaks of the joy of life. But I hate to see men and women lying on the ground and kissing in public.

I love the Negro porters, messengers, and elevator boys, sporting wherever they are, with their sharp winks and sly smiles, but I profoundly commiserate with the serious-looking Negroes going about with their gloves, spats, and their civilization.

I like the smile of sweet New England ladies, speaking in heavenly accents, and detest the sight of people in subways constantly moving their jaws up and down, without any smoke ever coming out.

I like subways, carrying me so fast, provided they carry me to my destination. But I feel humiliated to see blonde girls in high-heeled shoes overtaking me at my fastest pace. Holy Moses! Where is she going?

I love the sight of morning rides in subways, when the lines around men's and women's eyes have been gently smoothed out by sweet slumber and there is a twinkle in their looks. But I always feel highly uncomfortable during the afternoon rides, when the facial lines are so sharp, the eyes so harsh, and the faces so taut-drawn.

Sometimes I catch glimpses of sweet, calm faces, dignified faces and soulful faces; and then a discordant note comes, and they pass by. And I am left in the midst of eyes staring with a glinting glare and chins sticking out, speaking of a desperate ambition to achieve, and voices without soft modulation.

And I see middle-aged housewives returning with packages from Macy's or Wanamaker's, chatting, chatting, chatting about the awful realities of life with an awful awareness, and they do my heart good, because they remind me of China. And I see once in a while a sweet, pensive, lonely girl talking to no one and wish I could penetrate into her soul's yearnings.

I see white-haired and ruddy-faced old men, who survey this tide of humanity, I suspect, very much as I do. Then I see with a shock other old men, apologetic for being old and continually protesting by their manner that they are still young in spirit.

I always feel tremendously amused that, even in America, men do not always rise to give a lady a seat. But I feel enraged when an old man is left standing.

I am interested in the quintuplets as a curiosity, but am stunned at the way they have been turned to commercial purpose. I admire the Lindberghs and feel sorry for them that the cameramen persecuted them. I am a disciple of American democracy and enthusiastic about civil rights and liberties. But I am amazed that there isn't an amendment to the American Constitution, protecting every American citizen from facing cameramen and reporters against his will and guaranteeing him the right of privacy, the only right that makes life worth living.

I admire the gentleman in America and feel sorry for him that he has to be ashamed of his culture and his better opinions—feel sorry that he has been cudgeled into conformity, caged in silence, and haunted by the fear of being different from the common man. I understand but nevertheless wonder at the fairly complete absence of gentlemen from politics.

I pay tribute to American democracy and American toleration. I enjoy the liberty with which American newspapers criticize their public officials and admire the American officials for taking public criticism with a gracious sense of humor.

I am always touched by American business courtesy and the liberal use of "thank you's." But I am always amused at the "Oh, yeah's?" which are a cliché to hide the vacuity of the speaker's intellect.

I love dinners under subdued lights and the quiet appointments of good American homes, but I always come home a mental wreck from cocktail parties, at which one attains the maximum physical movement with the minimum mental activity. A cocktail party is a place where you talk with a person you do not know about a subject you have no interest in. It is like taking ten wrong trains and coming back ten times from Manhattan Transfer, finally landing in Pennsylvania Station after an hour of completely wasted, purposeless activity.

A cocktail party is also an institution where you learn simultaneously to wave your hand to someone across the room on your right, smile a greeting to someone on your left, and manage to say, "Oh, yeah?" to the lady in front, with whom you are supposed to be engaged in a philosophic conversation.

I appreciate the sentiments of Soup Magnates and Pork Kings and Bristle Heiresses importing entire English castles and French chateaux brick by brick, but I have other opinions about office buildings inspired by factories and residences inspired by office buildings. In fact, I see only business executives working in factory buildings and men and women residing in office buildings, but I have never seen American families living in homes in the City of New York.

I admire the American love for old furniture and old carpets but am sorry to find chromium taking the place of wood in the home. Chromium is too cold for the home and too hard for the soul. Something terribly akin I see between platinum blondes and chromium homes and tin-can souls.

I am delighted at servidors, refrigerators, vacuum carpet cleaners, and escalators, but I hate to look at a bed that springs down from what seems to be a wardrobe door. I like labor-saving devices but hate all space-saving inventions.

The American home developed from chimneyed cottages, was changed into apartment flats, and is disappearing into the trailer. The trailer is the logical development of the American home from the apartment flat, which has been defined as the place where some members of the family wait for the return of the car being occupied by other members of the family. So why not build a slightly bigger car in which all the members can live all the time? The American will soon be living in partitioned cracker barrels, if he doesn't look out!

4

THE CHINESE AND THE JAPANESE

WHAT is happening in the Far East reveals strikingly the great difference between the Chinese and the Japanese. These differences must be understood if we are to forecast with any accuracy future developments in the Chinese-Japanese drama.

Japan and China are racial entities which refuse to be snugly put away with certain labels or formulas. Racial traits are a highly complex subject. Sometimes even contradictory traits are found in the same nation, because such traits are the products of different streams of influence in the nation's history in the same period or at different periods.

One of the strangest phenomena, which has puzzled me for some time, is the differences between Japanese and Chinese humor. In art and literature the Japanese have shown a fine sense of humor; they have an original type of humorous literature ("Barber-shop Chats" and "Bath Chats"), which compares favorably with, if it does not excel, Chinese humor. And yet in action and in national life the Japanese seem to behave essentially like the humorless Germans—they are clumsy, heavy, stupidly logical, and hopelessly bureaucratic. On the other hand, the Chinese are an essentially humorous people in their daily life, and yet in their classical literature the silent chuckle and ticklish laughter seem to be rare.

Here, then, we have contradiction and inconsistency in the same nation, undoubtedly to be accounted for in this instance by literary tradition. The trouble is that things are not always simple when viewed at close range. Just imagine the home of Puritanism being the birthplace of the broad academic freedom represented by Harvard!

With this warning against facile generalizations, let us look at Chinese and Japanese racial traits and observe their differences and similarities. For the Chinese and the Japanese are different enough to make them disagreeable neighbors and similar enough to intensify their hearty dislike of each other. Like Americans and their English cousins, we hate to see ourselves resembling each other so much. But that is the beauty of life: to find similarities in differences and rich varieties in a common stock. Not that the Japanese are racially related to ours; the Japanese tongue does not even belong in the Indo-Chinese family.

First let me point out the similarities between the two

peoples. In many visible aspects of civilization the Japanese are similar to the Chinese, for Japan was a fairly apt pupil of China. Up to the modern period the whole structure of Japanese civilization, as we usually understand the term, was essentially Chinese and imported from China.

China gave Japan her pottery, painting, silk, lacquer, printing, writing, copper coins, paper windows, lanterns, firecrackers, bonfires, Buddhist Zen philosophy, Sung philosophy, Confucian monarchism, Tang poetry, the art of tea drinking, tasting spring water, cultivating flowers, pavilions, and the rock garden. China also gave Japan many of her national festivals: for instance, the fifteenth of the first moon, the seventh of the seventh moon, and the ninth of the ninth moon. I am not so sure but that China taught the Japanese to admire fireflies.

China certainly taught Japan to train better housewives, to imbue them with more courtesy, more meekness, and more selfless devotion than China could impart to her own daughters. The only thing that China could not teach, and the Japanese could not absorb, was the subtle "do-nothing" philosophy of Taoism. The Japanese have not got Taoist blood in them, and educational philosophy tells us that there is no use trying to bring out something in a person which is not originally there. This results in the most amazing difference between the Japanese and the Chinese, for, while the Japanese are perfectionists, the Chinese are a nation of happy-go-lucky individuals. The implications of such a difference are far-reaching, especially in an industrial age.

The Japanese in the past have done well with some of the things they learned from China and not so well with others. In their entire history they have not produced a single philosopher. But in many other things they rival and often surpass their masters. In the field of art, which includes poetry, painting, flower arrangement, and house decoration, they have essentially caught the Chinese spirit, have kept that spirit alive when China has forgotten it, and have in many instances created styles and genres of their own. In this field of Oriental art (which I may summarize as a characteristic appreciation of transient poetic moods and the beauty of the commonplace, small things of life) the Japanese are past masters in their own way. The development of the seventeen-word poem as a verse form (for expressing, or rather barely suggesting, a mood, a sentiment) testifies to their mastery.

> *Swat not that fly: he is rubbing his hands and feet.*

or:

> *The sound of a green frog leaping into an ancient pool.*

—That is as Chinese in feeling as any Chinese poem can be, or perhaps even more so.

In the development of the humorous tale or sketch, as I have already said, the Japanese owe nothing to Chinese patterns—the creation of a character, for example, in a travel sketch in which the rascal picks up a string of cash from under the seat cushion of a sedan chair, says nothing about it and hides it in his sleeves, and then grandiloquently takes it out to pay for the drinks of his friends.

That humor, too, is found in the cartoons of the Japanese, of which they have a very rich and varied tradition of 800 years, and in their now famous woodcuts. The feeling in the cartoon sketches and woodcuts is still a sensitive feeling for the ordinary doings of ordinary people in daily life—a pair of chess players so absorbed in their game that a child has been able to put something on the head of one of the players without his knowing it; or the expression on the face of a poor schoolmaster accidentally hit on the head with a ball by school children at play. These are the things that Japanese artists delight in, and in that they are more Chinese than the Chinese artists.

How can I help paying tribute to the Japanese artistic sense and poetic sentiment when the Japanese have understood and felt and expressed so well what is in ourselves? They have, above all, understood the beauty of simplicity, that beauty of simplicity seen so well in Japanese interiors, corresponding to the Chinese ideal of "a clean, bare desk before a clear window," and seen also in their sheer delight in clean-scrubbed, unvarnished wood surfaces.

If I were to express in a few words the differences between the Japanese and the Chinese, I should say that the Japanese lack the reasonable spirit, the broadness of view, the pacifism, and the democracy of the Chinese. These traits all hang together. The Japanese have more loyalty to the Emperor and to the State, more discipline, more determination to get on in this life, and—here is a surprising result—more ceremonialism than the Chinese. The Japanese are busier, but the Chinese are wiser.

My opinion may be due to my being a Chinese, but I feel that when you look for depth and creative originality—the final tests of the cultural work of a great nation—the Japanese record is disappointing. Depth and creative originality, however, are not required by a nation in order to get on, for the world is full of people who have no depth and no originality and yet get on swimmingly. It is of those somewhat luxurious aspects of culture that I am speaking. In art, it comes out as the phenomenon that so many Japanese things are pretty, and so few beautiful. The Japanese have understood delicacy, a kind of insular delicacy, and they understand perhaps more than any other nation the beauty of miniatures and the small, the light, the tiny. But I am still looking for a feeling for mystic depth and grandeur in their art. So far my general impression is that everything is as light and shaky as their wooden houses.

Can the phrase, "the reasonable spirit"—that mother of spiritual mellowness—explain or cover the differences mentioned? Perhaps it can. The Japanese warlike spirit, Japanese determination, Japanese fanatical loyalty to the Emperor, and Japanese high-strung nationalism, are all expressions of the lack of the reasonable spirit. No one who is reasonable can be warlike; no one who is reasonable can be determined; no one who is reasonable can be a fanatic.

The Chinese are too reasonable to be warlike, too reasonable to be determined, too reasonable to subscribe to any form of fanaticism, and too reasonable to be good hundred-per-centers. The final appeal of any disputing parties arguing in the Chinese language is: "Now is this reasonable?" The party who admits being unreasonable is already defeated and condemned.

This reasonable spirit tempers, for instance, Chinese ceremonialism, the Chinese attitude toward women and toward monarchy. The Chinese are supposed to be highly ceremonial in their intercourse, and that supposition is highly erroneous, arrived at because foreigners derive exaggerated notions from the Chinese idioms of address, which do not mean anything to the Chinese because they are only idioms.

The Chinese are in fact about the free-est in their ways

among all the peoples I know—free-est because they are the most happy-go-lucky. They are irked by the Japanese cere-monialism of drinking tea. Japanese women still learn in their modern girls' normal schools how to bow and crawl properly. Just try to teach Chinese girls to bow today—it is unimaginable!

The Chinese gave women a lower position, but at least they recognize it as unreasonable when they see Japanese husbands bring sing-song girls home and expect their wives to serve and entertain them, which the Japanese wives so graciously do, or used to do. And Chinese women do not use a different language of self-abnegation in addressing men, as Japanese women do, even when Japanese mothers address their sons.

And so the Confucian system of subjection of women to men, of the common people to the aristocracy, and of the sub-jects to the Emperor, attained in Japan a rigor which it never attained in China. The Japanese worship of the Emperor cannot but seem like fanaticism to the Chinese, a fanaticism which undoubtedly works for national strength, but which, after all, is made possible by absence of thinking. And Japan developed the samurai caste which China did not develop. In the end, this so worked out that even under the Chinese monarchy the spirit was essentially democratic.

The amazing thing is that, in spite of 2,000 years of his-tory, with all the changes of the shogunate, Japan has one continuous, unbroken imperial dynasty, while China has had over twenty. Even in the periods of turmoil and feudal wars, when the Japanese Emperor's power dwindled to noth-ing, as in 1336-1392 and 1467-1583, the imperial lineage and the dynastic throne were left intact. In short, Japanese mon-archs assumed a semi-divine character which Chinese mon-archs never acquired. The Chinese were too reasonable to accept that character, and the Chinese historians evolved the theory that the Emperor held the throne in trust from Heaven, and forfeited his right as soon as he misruled, and thus the right to rebellion was vindicated. That would be "dangerous thought" in Japan.

Some time ago, a Japanese university professor of political science created a national and cabinet crisis by making the academic statement that "the Emperor is an organ of the State and not the State itself." The professor, as I remember, had ultimately to retract that statement. Such a form of thinking is utterly imaginable to the Chinese.

This essentially explains that greater cohesion of Japan as a nation. There is no question that the Japanese are a nation of more orderly and better disciplined individuals. Try to tell a Chinese the benefit of cohesion and the virtue of discipline, and he just smiles behind his long sleeves.

You cannot make a philosophic individualist into a good citizen. As the world is constituted at present, with fierce national conflicts, probably it would be better to have hundred-percenters and A-1 patriots than to have reasonable individuals living reasonable lives. And the Chinese probably will eventually adjust themselves to that. But they will do so only out of condescension toward the world into which they have had the bad luck to be born. You have to do a good deal of preaching to convince the Chinese of the beauty of national greatness. You can tell him to watch a swanky parade or an awe-inspiring fleet, and he will admit it is beautiful to look at, but you cannot get much further with him. To have a fleet to look at: that is a beautiful idea.

So it seems to me that the Japanese are supremely fitted to become a warlike Fascist nation, moving like a machine, and the Chinese are supremely unfit to become the same. The trouble is that the Chinese thinks too much as an individual, and you cannot make a Fascist nation, moving by goose step, out of thinking individuals. It just does not make sense for human beings to move by goose step.

My suspicion is that thought control in Japan is somewhat superfluous, because all Japanese think alike anyway.

This explains what I mean by the greater spirit of reasonableness, the broadness of view, and the greater democracy and pacifism of the Chinese. After all, the Chinese overthrew their last imperial dynasty, but the Japanese dynasty will apparently last forever. It has, at least theoretically, lasted nearly 2,000 years, going back straight to the Sun Goddess.

There is no use trying to belittle modern Japan. Japan's sudden, meteoric rise to a world power is no accident. National cohesion, discipline, capacity for organization, and capacity for adaptation (or imitation, if you like), the martial spirit, and a great capacity for hard work—these are great qualities. To show that there is real national strength in Japan, it is perhaps more pertinent to point out that her annual output of books exceeds those of America and of England, and is exceeded only by those of Russia and Germany.

But in the lack of the "reasonable spirit," of mellowness, subtlety, and free criticism, lies also the danger to modern Japan. Japan has goose-stepped into the front rank of nations, but goose-stepping while marking time is extremely tiring, and goose-stepping forever without a little thinking is dangerous.

Japan has undoubtedly got to the front rank. She has got there, it seems to me, by sheer force of character but without much thinking. The reforms of Emperor Meiji transformed

Japan into a modern nation by the goose-stepping process. It was a remarkable example of what happens when you put modern weapons, industrial, scientific, and military, into the hands of a small, compact, cohesive island people, with the ready-made martial, loyal, nationalistic spirit of a feudal society.

Japan swallowed Western civilization whole, its militarism, its capitalism, its nationalism, and its belief in power, and superimposed it upon a feudalistic society with no time to think for itself. That gave her civilization a machinelike, humorless, inhuman quality. This machinelike humorless quality is seen in the bothersome, routine-loving, and perfectly serious Japanese customs officials and police; the vainglorious dreams of the army, and the cockiness of a "Japan-uber-Alles" diplomatic challenge to the world, including Great Britain.

I am sure this cockiness must often give Prince Saionji and a few other elderly statesmen a heartache. Through her complete and unmitigated cockiness of tone and attitude Japan wriggled herself into a position of international isolation, and then picked up Fascist Germany for her ally, somewhat to her own consternation. That illustrates what I mean by Japanese lack of subtlety. Sheer belief in power does not always get results.

I am sorry to say that Japan has even lost her *bushido,* that admirable spirit of chivalry. And I should have expected the Japanese to have more subtlety than to demand that the Chinese suppress a perfectly natural anti-Japanese feeling, brought about by Japan's own acts, and certainly more subtlety than to send warships and bombers to stamp out the anti-Japanese feeling. That the Japanese are perfectly sincere and desirous of stamping out this anti-Japanese feeling is beyond question, and their seriousness about it makes it seem so tragic. They do not realize that there are certain things that even a bomber cannot stamp out. In fighting against anti-Japanese feeling they are fighting nature's law of action and reaction, and it is idiotic to fight against nature. Even guns cannot fight against nature.

So the net result is that Japan is accomplishing in China the opposite of what she set out to do. The most unpleasant side of Japanese character, unfortunately, is dominant and politically effective in present-day Japan—that side of Japanese character which is represented by the Japanese militarists. The Japanese liberal elements certainly see the folly of "riding a tiger" and swashbuckling—riding toward ruin when greater and more stable results might be achieved by softer means.

A final rapprochement between China and Japan is imaginable only if there is a domestic change in the Japanese Government and the civil leaders gain control over the military. Failing that, even the best war machine in the world cannot save the Japanese from nature's law of action and reaction.

5

HIROTA AND THE CHILD

A CHILD'S GUIDE to Sino-Japanese Politics:

The Child: Daddy, who's coming to tea this afternoon?
Hirota: Wang Chunghui.
The Child: Who is Wang Chunghui?
Hirota: He is a Chinese.
The Child: Do you make friends with the Chinese, Daddy?
You told me the Chinese are not half as good as
the Japanese. My teacher told me all sorts of
nasty things about the Chinese every day.

Hirota: Will you shut up?

The Child: May I come, too? I want to see this Wang Chunghui.

Hirota: Dearie, I would let you, if you didn't have that awful habit of asking questions. But today, we are going to talk about Sino-Japanese relations. You won't understand.

The Child: Are Sino-Japanese relations very difficult to understand?

Hirota: Very.

The Child: Why is it very difficult to understand?

Hirota: We want to make friends with the Chinese, but they don't want to make friends with us.

The Child: Why? Do they hate us?

Hirtoa: They do. They hate us more than they hate the Europeans.

The Child: Why is that? Have we been worse to them than the Europeans?

Hirota: Now, will you stop twisting that string around your fingers!

The Child: But why do they hate us if we have been good friends with them?

Hirota: The "Manchukuo."

The Child: Is "Manchukuo" their country or our country?

Hirota: Now, you are monkeying with that string again. You are dropping fibers on the carpet.

The Child: How are you going to be friends with the Chinese?

Hirota: We will lend them money and we will give them advisers.

The Child: Don't they have European advisers already? Do

the Europeans want to make friends with the Chinese, too? Will they lend China money?

Hirota: They will, but we must not let them. Sonny, you must understand: When they lend money to China, they will dominate China.

The Child: And when we lend them money?

Hirota: When we lend them money, it is to make friends with them and help them.

The Child: Then the Chinese will take money from us rather than from the Europeans.

Hirota: No, they won't, unless we force them to take our help.

The Child: That is very funny. Why do you force them to take our help, if they don't want it?

Hirota: Don't stick your finger in your mouth. And you haven't seen the dentist yet!

The Child: Very well, but, Daddy, do you think, if you were a Chinese, you would trust the Japanese?

Hirota: You see, dear, we haven't been exactly friends with them. But now, we will make friends with them; we will lend them money and we will give them advisers and we will police their country and put the country in order for them. We want to make them see the *real* intentions of our country.

The Child: What are the *real* intentions of our country?

Hirota: You idiot! I told you already. I want to make Wang Chunghui see that we really want to help them this afternoon.

The Child: Is Wang Chunghui an idiot?

Hirota: How dare you! He is a very great jurist and a very learned man.

The Child: Shall I grow up to be a Wang Chunghui?

Hirota: You may try, if you work hard at your lessons.

The Child: Suppose I am Wang Chunghui, how are you going to tell me the real intentions of our country?

Hirota: Why, Sonny, I would tell you how we are going to lend you money and give you military advisers and police your country and put your country in order.

The Child: Tell me, Daddy, why do you really want to do all this? Can't you let China alone?

Hirota: You see, we want to capture the entire Chinese trade and drive out all the Europeans from China. We can sell a lot to them, and they can buy a lot from us. That is good, for this Pan-Asiaticism is very good. And we must get China to fight on our side against the Russians. We haven't got iron, we haven't got cotton, we haven't got rubber, and we haven't got enough food supply in case of war to last more than twelve months if we don't get China on our side. We must fight Russia in China.

The Child: You won't tell Wang Chunghui all this, will you?

Hirota: As a diplomat's son, I think it is time that you learned this. We diplomats never say what we mean, but all of us have learned to read each other's lies very accurately. Wang Chunghui hasn't got to be told.

The Child: How clever! But what are you going to call it?

Hirota: We are going to call it the ushering in of a new era of Sino-Japanese co-operation on the basis of "common existence and common prosperity" in the interests of the maintenance of peace in Asia and the world.

The Child: Oh, I'm all excited! How wonderful it all sounds! Where did you learn all this? Do they teach us at school to say awful things as beautifully as that?

Hirota: That is what the school is teaching you every day in your composition class. But a diplomat is born, not taught.

The Child: Oh, how wonderful you are, Daddy! But suppose Wang Chunghui sees all that you really mean, and all his countrymen, too, and refuse to be helped by us, how are you going to capture the Chinese trade? What are you going to do about it?

Hirota: The Imperial Army will see to that.

The Child: But this is not really being friendly with China, is it? They will hate us all the more. Do you like the Imperial Army methods?

Hirota: (*Quickly*) Hush! Hush! Don't let anybody hear you. I think you'd better trot along and see the dentist. . . . And don't throw your pencil ends and strings about the floor!

(*The Child picks up his string and pencil end from the floor, sticks them in his pocket, and leaves the room. Hirota heaves a sigh of relief.*)

6

"OH, BREAK NOT MY WILLOW TREES!"

"OH, BREAK not my willow trees!" Somehow the line lingers in my ears. It begins one of the loveliest love songs from the *Book of Poetry* that I learned in childhood. Reading in *Tien Hsia* monthly an article by John C. H. Wu, I came across an English translation by J. A. Carpenter. Carpenter's translation, which has been set to music by Cyril Scott, preserves the original charm. This is what an ancient Chinese girl said to her lover:

> Don't come in, Sir, please,
> Don't break my willow trees!
> Not that *that* would very much grieve me;
> But alack-a-day! what would my parents say?
> And love you as I may,
> I cannot bear to think what that would be.
>
> Don't cross my wall, Sir, please,
> Don't spoil my mulberry trees!
> Not that *that* would very much grieve me;
> But alack-a-day! what would my brothers say?
> And love you as I may,
> I cannot bear to think what that would be.

There is still a third stanza, but these will suffice to show the freshness and vigor of ancient Chinese poetry. It is Elizabethan.

Perhaps the line is haunting my ears because a neighbor of mine has recently been breaking my willow trees. For I have a very big garden, an old, old garden. It is the garden of my ancestors, and for generations and generations we have lived in it. My neighbor on the northeast who is a social upstart, has been climbing over my walls and carrying on a shameless flirtation with my daughter, and it pains me to see those old, old willow trees broken and trampled upon as a result of their shameless love making, as in the love song of old. In fact, he has not only broken my willow trees, but has broken into my garden and stolen a large patch of my orchard on the northeast, and that is why I am writing about him now.

My neighbor who lives on the northeast is a typical upstart bourgeois. In fact, his is an interesting case of upstart psychology. His name is James Alexander Lapps. Before his rise to fortune, he used to sign himself merely "J.A." but now it is "James Alexander." To us, his neighbors, however, he is

known merely as "Fisher Lapps" from his profession, and
Sophia, their northwestern neighbor, persists in calling Mr.
Lapps "Fisher Lapps" which annoys Mr. and Mrs. Lapps
greatly.

Fisher Lapps inevitably goes to church with his entire
family. Since his rise to fortune, he has also bought a pew in
the same row with J. P. Morgan. For the life of me, I can't
see what fun he has worshiping God from the same row as
J. P. Morgan, for I notice his hours at church are a veritable
torture. Mrs. Lapps is as scared as she is delighted at sitting
in the same row with Mrs. Morgan. She is all the time studying Mrs. Morgan's dress and watching how Mrs. Morgan
blows her nose. The Lapps family sail up to the church in
their Rolls-Royce, conscious that they are newly accepted
members of high society, and Fisher is blamelessly correct,
for he has bought a book of social etiquette and gone over it
three times point by point. He has mastered the entire book
of etiquette in an amazingly short time, and there is no deny-
ing his intelligence, for after all no fisherman can rise to a
position of wealth and influence without some real pluck
and intelligence.

Fisher Lapps forgets only one thing, that no gentleman
ever observes all the rules of social etiquette, with the result
that Fisher Lapps is too blamelessly correct to appear a
natural-born gentleman. There are things like kindness and
simplicity and subtlety and finesse which are not in the book
of etiquette and which Fisher Lapps consequently could
never learn. Fisher has the most correct and yet the worst
possible manners. For all the solicitous desire to appear
blamelessly correct and Mrs. Lapps's rather too prominently
displayed jewels, Lapps's wife is feeling extremely uncomfortable, partly because of her self-consciousness about her

new wealth and partly because Mrs. Morgan has an utter contempt for her and she knows it, too. Mrs. Morgan tells the other women that she does not mind the fisherwoman's jewels, but she can't stand Fisher Lapps's top hat and white gloves, because she says no one wears white gloves at church. Mrs. Morgan and the other old parishioners accept them and yet do not accept them, but Fisher Lapps has a way of flaunting his wealth before the eyes of his fellow parishioners, and his new Rolls-Royce always makes a real impression on them, in spite of their contempt for what they call behind Fisher's back a "contemptible cad" and a "social climber."

Once he used to joke with J. P. Morgan. Now joking is one of the few amenities of life that take long years of cultivation. Fisher Lapps meant to be humorous. One day, coming out of the church, he patted Mr. Morgan on the shoulders and said, "Hullo! J. P. You are J. P. and I am J. A. Ha! ha! ha! How funny!"

Mr. Morgan merely froze him with a "How do you do, Fisher." Evidently Mr. Morgan did not think it so funny.

Fisher Lapps apologized (for you could not find a more courteous person on earth) and then walked away, swinging his stick according to the book of etiquette. You can tell that swinging a stick is not natural to him. "For God's sake!" Mrs. Pierce used to curse at such a sight.

Mrs. Lapps is now speaking English. She has even learned an Americanism, "I'll tell the world!" It is that swaggering "I'll tell the world!" of hers that got on everybody's nerves. She learned it from her husband and her children learned it from her and now the little Lapps are always saying "I'll tell the world!" when they are not bowing and saying, "So sorry!" The entire Lapps family being rather short of stature, the effect is a supreme comedy.

The upshot of it all is, the Lapps merely succeed in being disliked by everybody.

We have been neighbors for generations. He was a poor fellow, plying a fisherman's trade, and we an old, old aristocratic family. In my father's mansion there is a huge orchard with a great variety of flowers and fruit trees. But our family has fallen on evil days, and the orchard is now in a dilapidated state. For all that, our family has still an utter contempt for the Lapps and the Lapps know it, too. My neighbor has been peeping over the wall at our garden for years, and there is covetousness in his heart. And now his son has the audacity to sue for the hand of my daughter who lives in the northeastern courtyard of my garden. It is because of this shameless courtship with my daughter that he is now constantly breaking into my garden and breaking my willow trees.

Some years ago he went abroad and mysteriously returned with rolls and bags of silver. Like all *nouveaux riches,* he began to tear down his old house and build a new one and then began to complain of lack of space. Around their fireside, Fisher's wife always discussed with her husband what their neighbors' houses looked like and how their own house ought to look, as a first step toward entry into high society. "Push" and energy? Yes, the Lapps have got it. It was inevitable that he should cast covetous eyes at my centuries-old garden, and particularly at the adjoining northeastern patch of fruit trees and flower trees. I had too big a garden anyway, they used to remark at home among themselves. It was then that he began to call himself my good neighbor and to take a deep interest in my daughter. My daughter marrying a Lapps!

Fisher Lapps wants my garden and he knows it, too. But

being fundamentally ill-bred, he is terribly afraid of being socially incorrect in stealing it. He is anxious to steal and still more anxious to wear his top hat and go to church. Consequently he has developed a certain technique of stealing which amuses everybody except himself. For the one thing that a social upstart hasn't got and does not pretend to have is a sense of humor. Humor comes from self-confidence and taking things easy, and Fisher Lapps can't take things easy. One thing he can't forget is his "honor" and he is known to be terribly "sensitive." Of course, a fisherman in a Rolls-Royce cannot help being sensitive.

The encroachment on my property began with a little kite incident. Before Fisher became rich, he never flew kites. But since then he has developed a craze for flying kites. One day one of his kites was flying over my garden and was caught in a tree branch. Like the respectable member of society that he is, he came over and spoke to me, "How dare your tree catch my kite? I must have it cut down. If you don't do it yourself, I will cut it down for you. I'll tell the world!" My son allowed him to go ahead, and I'm too old a man to bother.

Since the first kite was caught and the first tree was cut down, a regular series of "kite incidents" has begun to follow, for it seemed then inevitable that every week a new kite must be flown and caught and another of my trees must be chopped down. Having broken over my fence and trampled upon my willow trees near the fence, he would begin flying kites from the last felled willow trees and the kites would begin a habit of being caught farther and farther inside my garden. Always it was the next tree nearer my house that was the great nuisance. By this time almost my entire northeastern garden is occupied by him, and today he is flying kites right over the wall of my northeastern court. But he goes about telling all our parishioners that my trees were wrong and his kites were right, that it was the audacity of my trees in catching his kites which injured his bourgeois honor and compelled him to "punish" me by occupying a large patch of my garden. He is so sensitive about his "honor" that you could almost think that he believes it himself. And so after church service, when Mrs. Lapps declares to Mrs. Morgan and other parishioners her rather sudden "friendship" with me and her love for me as a neighbor, they barely succeed in concealing their laughter out of respect for her Rolls-Royce and her abnormal sense of "honor."

It was some time after this, last spring I believe, that young Lapps began to woo my profligate daughter who is now occupying my northeastern courtyard, and I am too old a man to bother, either. Like the old lover in the ancient *Book of Poetry,* he is this very day breaking my willow trees and mulberry trees in my northeastern courtyard. Sometimes I feel like saying to Fisher, "Oh, break not my willow trees!" or giving him a piece of my mind, but I am an old man, and oh, what's the use? Besides, does it really matter? Now, he has taken upon himself the duty of changing alleyways and dictating who is to do what in that northeastern courtyard, as if it were his own property. And all the time he is talking about his "honor" and never knows how funny it sounds in other people's ears. Since this affair with my daughter began, he is a still greater friend of mine than before and he professes his good neighborly feelings for me more vociferously than ever.

My son, to avoid trouble, is returning his calls and takes every occasion to declare to Fisher Lapps his reciprocal friendship. It is often at one of these calls at Fisher's house that my son receives a stern rebuff.

"I love you," my son would say. "You are the best neighbor I have."

"Tut!" Lapps would reply. "You are insincere! Why do you obstruct my son's courtship with your sister? Where is the evidence of your friendship?"

"But I do approve of my sister's marriage," reiterated my son most vehemently.

"Impossible! I can't believe that your people approve of their daughter marrying a Lapps!" said old Lapps.

Fisher is right. I can't possibly be "sincere" when I profess my "friendship." His instinct tells him so.

If Fisher Lapps were a downright thief, he would have said, "If you give me your house, then I will believe in your friendship." But, being as I said a *nouveau riche* and terribly afraid of being socially incorrect, he just stopped short of that. But to my son his meaning is perfectly clear. He wants not only my outer garden on the northeast; he wants my courtyard within the wall.

And so Lapps and my young son would often come out of the church hand in hand like great friends and everybody would look on with an amused smile. And now when I have got a son like that, what am I going to live for?

7

CAPTIVE PEKING

PEKING is to Nanking as Kyoto is to Tokyo. Both Peking
and Kyoto are ancient capitals, around which hang an aroma
and mystery and historic charm which the younger capitals,
Nanking and Tokyo, cannot possibly have. Nanking (before
1938) and Tokyo stand for the modern age, for progress, in-
dustrialism, and nationalism, while Peking stands for the
soul of old China, cultured and placid; for the good life and
good living, and for an arrangement of life in which the

maximum comforts of civilization are brought into perfect harmony with the maximum beauty of the rural life.

That is why, if you ask a Chinese who knows both Nanking and Peking which one is closer to his heart, there is no question that Peking will be the choice. That is also why a man—let him be Chinese, Japanese, or European—who has lived in Peking for a year wouldn't want to live in any other city in China. For Peking is one of the jewel cities of the world. Except Paris and (by hearsay) Vienna as they once were, there is no city in the world that is quite so nearly ideal, in regard to nature, culture, charm, and mode of living, as Peking.

I am not discussing here the right and wrong of Japanese occupation of Peking, or questions of "provocations," "self-defense," "stabilization of the Far East," or the general righteousness and love of peace of the Japanese Army. Every time the Japanese rain bombs and machine-gun bullets along with handbills protesting their affection for their "beloved friends," the Chinese people—the warlike Chinese—become unaccountably more and more scared of friendship and wish less and less the "stabilization of the Far East." But you seldom hear China talking of "self-defense," because China hasn't got a navy to sail up the Japan Sea. When she can do that, you may be quite sure that China will bomb Kyoto's civilian population just to defend herself and regard the presence of Japanese troops in Tokyo as a threat to peace in the Far East! As it is, the presence of Chinese troops in Peking is decidedly "provocative" and a threat to peace in Asia. So we will not discuss that now.

Peking is like a grand old person, with a grand old personality. For cities *are* like persons, with their different personalities. Some are mean and provincial, curious, and inquisitive; others are generous, magnanimous, big-hearted, and cosmopolitan. Peking is magnanimous. Peking is big. She harbors the old and the modern, being unmoved herself.

Modern young misses in high-heeled shoes brush shoulders with Manchu ladies on wooden soles, and Peking doesn't care. Old painters with white, magnificent long beards live across the yard from young college students in their "public hostelries," (kungyü), and Peking doesn't care. Packards and Buicks compete with rickshas and mule carts and caravans, and Peking doesn't care.

Behind the towering Grand Hotel de Pékin is an alley where life proceeds as it has been doing for the last thousand years—who cares? A stone's throw from the magnificent Union Medical College, financed by the Rockefeller Foundation, are ancient curio shops with ancient curio dealers smoking their water pipes and doing business in their ancient ways—who cares? Dress your own style, pick your own restaurant, pursue your own hobby, follow love and beauty and truth, and practice shuttlecocks or violins—who cares?

Peking is like a grand old tree, whose roots stretch deep into the earth and draw sustenance from it. Living under its shade and subsisting upon its trunk and branches are millions of insects. How are the insects to know how big the tree is, how it grows, how far it reaches into the ground, and who are the insects living across on the other branch of the tree? How can a Peking resident describe Peking, so old and so grand?

One never feels that one knows Peking. After living there for ten years, one discovers in an alley an old crank, and regrets not having met him earlier; or a lovely old gentleman painter with a big, bare belly sitting on a bamboo chair under a great locust tree, fanning himself with a palm-leaf fan and dreaming his hours away; or an old shuttlecock player who can make the shuttlecock travel inch by inch on his head and drop flat on the sole of his shoe at the back; or a society of sword fencers; or a children's school of dramatics; or a ricksha coolie who turns out to be a member of a Manchu princely family; or a former magistrate of imperial times. How dare one say that one knows Peking?

"Peking is a jewel city, a jewel city such as the eyes of man have not seen before. It is a jewel city of golden and purple and royal blue roofs, of palaces and pavilions and lakes and parks and princes' gardens. It is a jewel set with the purple sides of Western Hills and the blue girdle of the Jade Fountain stream and centuries-old cedars looking down on human beings at the Central Park, the Temple of Heaven, and the Temple of Agriculture. In the city are nine parks and three imperial lakes, known as the "Three Seas," now thrown open to the public. And Peking has such a blue sky and such a beautiful moon, such rainy Summers, such cool, crisp Autumns, and such dry, clear Winters!

Peking is like a king's dream, with its palaces, princes' gardens, hundred-foot boulevards, art museums, colleges, universities, hospitals, temples, pagodas, and streets of art shops and second-hand book shops. Peking is like a gourmet's paradise. It has centuries-old restaurants, with old, smoky signboards, and wonderful waiters with shaved heads and towels across their shoulders, whose courtesy is perfect, since they were trained in the tradition of the imperial times and catered to high mandarin officials. It is a place for the rich and poor, where every neighborhood shop extends credit to a poor old resident, where peddlers sell delicacies cheaply, and where you can loll at a tea restaurant and kill an entire afternoon over a pot of tea.

Peking is the shoppers' heaven, being rich in China's old handicrafts—books, prints, paintings, curios, embroidery, jade, cloisonnés, lanterns. It is a place where you can shop at home, for dealers come to your doors with their wares, and in the early morning the alleys are filled with the most charming musical cries of hawkers.

Peking has quiet. It is a city of homes, where every house has a courtyard, and every courtyard has a jar of goldfish and a pomegranate tree, where vegetables are fresh, and pears are pears and persimmons are persimmons. It is the ideal city, where there is space for every one to breathe in, where rural quiet is matched with city comforts, where streets and alleys and canals are so arranged that one can find room for an orchard or a garden and glimpse the Western Hills while picking cabbage in the morning hours —a stone's throw from a big department store.

It has variety—variety of men. It has laws and breakers of laws, police and accomplices of police, thieves and protectors of thieves, beggars and kings of beggars. It has saints, sinners, Mohammedans, Tibetan "devil-expellers," fortune tellers, boxers, monks, prostitutes, Russian and Chinese taxi dancers, Japanese and Korean smugglers, painters, philosophers, poets, collectors of curios, young college students, and movie fans. It has political scoundrels, retired old magistrates, New Life followers, theosophists, wives of former Manchu officials, now serving as maids.

It has color—color of the old and color of the new. It has the color of imperial grandeur, of historic age and of Mongolian plains. Mongolian and Chinese traders come with their camel caravans from Kalgan and Nankow and pass through its historic gates. It has miles upon miles of city walls, forty or fifty feet broad at the gates. It has gate towers and drum towers, which announce the evenings for the residents. It has temples, old gardens, and pagodas, where every stone and every tree and every bridge have a history and a legend.

Of all the things that make Peking the ideal city to live in, I would single out three: first, its architecture; second, its mode of living; and, third, its common people.

The city dates back to the twelfth century, but in its present form it was built by the great Ming Emperor Yunglo in the beginning of the fifteenth century—Yunglo was the Emperor who rebuilt the Great Wall—and it was conceived in true imperial grandeur. There is a southern city, slightly smaller than the northern city, and from the outermost southern gate of the southern city reaches inward a central axis five miles long, passing through successive gates and leading up to the grand Throne Hall.

In the center of the northern city is the Forbidden City surrounded by moats and walls covered with golden-colored tiles and supported at the back by the Coal Hill, with its five pavilions with rainbow-colored roofs of glazed tile. Coal Hill affords a straight view down the central axis; near by is the Drum Tower. On the west and southwest side of the Forbidden City are the Three Seas, which were the private boating waters of the imperial family.

Parallel to the main axis are two broad avenues, Hatamen Street in the East City and Hsuanwumen Street in the West City, each about sixty feet wide, and joining them, running east and west before the Forbidden City, is the great Tienanmen Street, over a hundred feet wide. Out near the southern entrance of the outer city, on either side of the main axis are the Temple of Heaven and the Temple of Agriculture, where the Emperor used to pray for a good new year and a good harvest.

As the Chinese conception of architectural beauty is serenity, rather than sublimity, and as the palace roofs are of the low and broad sweeping type, and as nobody other than the Emperor was allowed to have houses with more than one story, the total effect is one of tremendous spaciousness.

Following up this vision of a central thoroughfare, and passing through its successive arched gates, one comes gradually to the main massive tower of the Forbidden City, after which marble terraces gradually lead up to the central Throne Hall. All along, the tourist catches under the crystal-blue sky glimpses of the palace roofs with their golden-colored glazed tiles.

But what makes Peking so charming is the mode of life, organized so that one can have peace and quiet, while living close to a busy street. Living is cheap and life is enjoyable for all. While officials and rich men can dine in big restaurants, a poor ricksha coolie can buy, with two coppers, a perfect assortment of oil, salt, pepper, and vinegar for his cooking purposes, with a few leaves of some spicy plant to boot. No matter where one lives, one's house is never so far away that there aren't a butcher shop, a grocery store, and a tea house in the near neighborhood.

And then, you are free, free to pursue your studies, your amusements, your hobbies, or your gambling and your politics. Nobody interferes and nobody cares a rap what you wear or what you do. Nobody asks questions. That is the bigness and cosmopolitanism of Peking. You can associate with saints or sinners, gamblers or scholars, painters or crooked politicians. If you are imperially minded, you can loiter round the palace and the Throne Hall and imagine yourself an emperor for a morning or afternoon.

But if you are poetic, you can wander in any of the nine parks around the city and spend an afternoon at tea tables, sitting on bamboo chairs, or inclining on rattan couches, beneath the cedar trees, spending no more than twenty-five cents. And be sure you will not be insulted by the always cheerful and courteous waiters.

Or of a summer afternoon, you can go to the Shihshahai Lake, half rice fields and half lotus ponds, where you can mix with the working people enjoying their leisure and watching boxers and jugglers. Or you can go out of the West Gate and saunter on the imperial highway leading to the Summer Palace under the shade of cool willow trees.

All around you are villages and wheat fields, with beggar children completely naked, who like to get a penny while playing on the roadside. You can start a chat with them, or you can close your eyes and pretend that you are asleep and hear the musical jingle of their voices gradually dying out behind you. Or you can go to the zoo, formerly a Manchu prince's garden, just outside the West Gate. Or you can wander among the ruins of the Italian Palace in the former Summer Palace, pillaged and burned down by European soldiers, and you cannot get a scene more dreary and forlorn. You are in the presence of God.

On journeying past the present Summer Palace, wherein you could spend an entire day, you pass scenes of idyllic beauty until you reach the Jade Fountain with its marble pagoda beckoning to you, where inside you can spend another leisurely afternoon, dipping your feet in its cool gurgling water of an emerald color. Or walking farther, you can go to the Western Hills and be lost there for an entire season.

The greatest charm of Peking is, however, the common people, not the saints and professors, but the ricksha coolies. Paying about a dollar for a trip by ricksha from the West City to the Summer Palace, a distance of five miles, you might think that you are getting cheap labor; that is correct, but you are not getting disgruntled labor. You are mystified by the good cheer of the coolies as they babble all the way among themselves and crack jokes and laugh at other people's misfortunes.

Or coming back to your home at night you might chance upon an old ricksha coolie, clothed in rags, who tells you his sad story of poverty and misfortunes with humor, refinement, and fatalistic good cheer. If you think he is too old to pull rickshas and want to get down, he will insist on pulling you to your home. But if you jump down and surprise him by giving the full fare, there's a lump in his throat and you are thanked as you have never been thanked before in your life.

8

A HYMN TO SHANGHAI

SHANGHAI is terrible, very terrible. Shanghai is terrible
in her strange mixture of Eastern and Western vulgarity,
in her superficial refinements, in her naked and unmasked
worship of Mammon, in her emptiness, commonness, and
bad taste. She is terrible in her denaturalized women, de-
humanized coolies, devitalized newspapers, decapitalized
banks, and denationalized creatures. She is terrible in her
greatness as well as in her weakness, terrible in her monstrosities, perversities, and inanities, terrible in her joys and
follies, and in her tears, bitterness, and degradation, terrible
in her vast immutable stone edifices that rear their heads

high on the Bund and in the abject huts of creatures subsisting on their discoveries from refuse cans. In fact, one
might sing a hymn to the Great Terrible City in the following fashion:

O Great and Inscrutable City. Thrice praise to thy greatness and to thy inscrutability!

Thrice praise to the city renowned for her copper odor
and her fat, oily bankers, with green-tinted skins and sticky
fingers;

To the city of hugging flesh and dancing flesh, of flat-
chested ladies fed on *jin-sen* soup and doves'-nest congee,
and still looking anemic and weary of life, in spite of their
jin-sen soup and doves'-nest congee;

To the city of eating flesh and sleeping flesh, of ladies
with bamboo-shoot feet and willow waists, rouged faces and
yellow teeth, cackling "He! he! he!" like monkeys from
their cradles to their graves;

To the city of running flesh and kowtowing flesh; of
hotel boys with shining, slippery heads and more slippery
manners, who minister to the fat, oily bankers with green-
tinted skins and sticky fingers and to the hugging flesh and
dancing flesh with rouged cheeks and yellow teeth;

Great and inscrutable art thou!

In the still hours of the night, one conjureth up a picture
of thy monstrosities; in the muddy stream of human traffic
on Nanking Road, muddier than the muddy fish of muddy
Whangpoo, one thinketh of thy greatness also;

One thinketh of thy successful, *pien-pien*-bellied mer-
chants, and forgetteth whether they are Italian, French,
Russian, English, or Chinese;

One thinketh of thy masseuses, naked dancers, Carlo Gar-
cias, and thy Foochow Road sing-song houses;

Of thy retired *tao-tai* and *tufei* and magistrates and generals, with tortoise-shell spectacles and roof-shaped mustaches, trying to court sing-song girls with their loot, and finding their love repulsed and their sexual hunger still unappeased after months of courtship;

Of the idiotic and half-witted sons of these retired *tao-tai* and generals, who help to rid them of their ill-gotten and sin-smelling wealth;

Of thy wealthy, degenerate opium smokers who parade the streets in Packard eights, guarded by robust well-fed, uniformed Russians;

Of thy Whangpoo River daily receiving its quota of would-be suicides, of thy dancing girls and heart-broken young men mingling with the muddy Whangpoo fish;

Of thy hotel tea balls, where vulgarity gathers to meet vulgarity and see how vulgarity dresses;

Of thy dog races, where white women in V-necked evening dress mingle merrily and rub shoulders with yellow shop apprentices and gray dogs and pink-eyed rabbits;

Of thy *nouveaux riches,* lost and giddy in the whirlpool of parties and rides, millionaires who order the hotel boys about like lieutenant colonels and eat their soup with their knives;

Of thy *nouveaux modernes,* intoxicated by a few phrases of *yang-ching-pang* pidgin and never letting an opportunity slip for saying "many thanks" and "excuse me" to you;

Of thy girl students sitting astride their baggage on the rickshas, with rolled socks and hats on which perch Robin Redbreasts and chrysanthemums of different colors;

Of thy haughty, ungentlemanly foreigners, so haughty and ungentlemanly that one knows where they belong in their own countries—men with a moderate head, but stiff

boots and strong calf muscles, who also make good use of
their stiff boots and strong calf muscles—

Men who give large tips and complain of exorbitant
prices, who feel legitimately aggrieved and insulted when
people fail to understand their native language;

One thinketh and wondereth of these things and faileth
to comprehend their whence or their whither.

O thou city that surpasseth our understanding! How impressive are thy emptiness and thy commonness and thy bad
taste!

Thou city of retired brigands, officials and generals and
cheats, infested with brigands, officials and generals and
cheats who have not yet made their fortunes!

O thou the safest place in China to live in, where even
thy beggars are dishonest!

9

WHAT I WANT

DIOGENES, the Corinthian philosopher, was once asked by Alexander what favor he would ask of the great conqueror, and his answer was a request that the conqueror stand a little aside so that he could enjoy his sunshine. This was the cynical man who went about in daytime with a lantern to look for an honest man. He had only one rough garment for winter and summer, and he slept and lived in a tub. Once he had a cup, but on learning that he could drink water from his hands, he threw it away, believing that by so doing, he had one less desire in this world.

Diogenes represents to us moderns an ideal very much opposite to ours, which seems to measure progress by the number of a man's wants and luxuries, and for that reason, the story always provokes some laughter and a certain envy. The fact is, we are very much in confusion as to what we really want. The modern man finds himself in continual perplexity in regard to many problems, and most of all in problems that affect most closely his personal life. The modern man cannot spare himself a certain luxurious envy for that ascetic ideal of Diogenes, and at the same time is far from willing to miss a really good moving picture show. That gives us the so-called "restlessness" of the modern spirit.

Now it is of course very easy to tear Diogenes to pieces. First of all, Diogenes lived in a gentle Mediterranean climate. No lady therefore need be ashamed that, living in a colder country than Greece, she wants a fur coat. Secondly, I do not respect any man who does not keep at least two sets of underwear, in case he sends one to the laundry. A Diogenes in the story book may exhale a certain spiritual fragrance, but a Diogenes as a bedfellow would be a different story. Thirdly, it is dangerous to teach our schoolboys that kind of ideal, since one of the prime aims of education is to teach them at least a love for books, for which Diogenes apparently did not care twopence. Fourthly, Diogenes lived in an age when the movies had not yet been invented and Mickey Mouse had not yet come to enrich our lives. Any man or boy who professes indifference to a Mickey Mouse cartoon is decidedly a mental degenerate and can be of no use to civilization. Generally, it is the man who has many wants and desires and hopes that lives a richer and more complete life, not the one who goes on in life, indifferent to what is around him. The tramp in the suburbs of London who does not admire and envy a smug fireside is decidedly a lower, not a higher, kind of animal.

The real charm of Diogenes for us lies in the fact that we moderns want too many things, and particularly that we often do not know what those things are. It is a trite saying that every society lady who goes the mad rounds of parties and pleasures soon is overcome by a feeling of utter boredom. A millionaire heiress who crosses the Atlantic four times a year from Paris to Buenos Aires, and back to the Riviera and Atlantic City, is of course only trying to escape from herself. And her male counterpart—I use the word "male" deliberately in the animal sense—has so many girl friends that he cannot even fall in love with one. That is the modern malady, which makes Diogenes sometimes appear like a hero to us.

In our best and sanest moments, however, we know that Diogenes' god cannot be our god, that we want a good many things in life, and that these things are definitely good for us. The man who knows what he wants is a happy man.

I think I know what I want. Here are the things that would make me happy. I shall not want other things.

I want a room of my own, where I can work. A room that is neither particularly clean nor orderly. No Mademoiselle Agathe to dust everything she can reach with her dust cloth. But a room comfortable and intimate and familiar. Over my couch hangs a Buddhist oil lantern, the kind you see before Buddhist or Catholic altars. An atmosphere full of smoke and the smell of books and unaccountable odors. On the shelf overlying the couch are books, a good variety of them, but not too many—only those I can read or have read with profit again and again, against the opinion of all the book reviewers of the world. None that takes too long to read, none that has a sustained argument, and none that has too much cold splendor of logic. They are books that I frankly and sincerely like. I would read Rabelais along with "Mutt and Jeff" and Don Quixote with "Bringing up Father." One or two Booth Tarkington, some cheap third-rate penny novels, some detective stories. None of those sentimental self-delineators for me. No James Joyce and no T. S. Eliot. My reason for not reading Karl Marx or Immanuel Kant is very simple: I can never get beyond the third page.

I want some decent gentlemen's clothing that I have worn for some time, and a pair of old shoes. I want the freedom to wear as little as I care to. While I do not go as far as Ku Ch'icnli, the famous scholar who read the classics naked, I must be allowed to go half naked in my own room when the temperature is ninety-five in the shade, and I shall not be ashamed to appear so before my servants. I want them to be as natural beings as myself. I want a shower bath in summer and a good fireside with logs burning in winter.

I want a home where I can be myself. I want to hear my wife's voice and the children's laughter upstairs when I am working downstairs, and downstairs when I am working upstairs. I want children who are children, who will go with me to play in the rain, and who enjoy a shower bath as much as I do. I want a patch of ground where my children can build brick houses and feed chickens, and water the flowers. I want to hear a cock crying *cock-a-doodle-do* in the morning. I want tall, old trees in the neighborhood.

I want some good friends, friends who are as familiar as life itself, friends to whom I need not be polite, and who will tell me all their troubles, matrimonial or otherwise, who can quote Aristophanes and crack some dirty jokes, friends who are spiritually rich and who can talk dirt and philosophy with the same candor, friends who have definite hobbies and opinions about persons and things, who have their private beliefs and respect mine.

I want a good cook, who knows how to cook vegetables

and make delicious soups. I want an old, old servant, who thinks I am a great man, but does not know where my greatness lies.

I want a good library, some good cigars, and a woman who understands and who leaves me free to do my work.

I want some bamboos in front of my study window, a rainy climate in summer, and a clear, blue sky in winter, such as we have in Peking.

I want the freedom to be myself.

10

WHAT I HAVE NOT DONE

IN ACCORDANCE with the great tradition of Chinese scholars, who always choose some poetic titles for their studies, I have also chosen one for mine, which is called *Yupuwei chai,* or "Have Not Done Studio." It is a rather longish title, but not half so long as another well-known studio, which is called "the Study Where You Look Up At One Thousand Seven Hundred and Twenty-Seven Storks." The direct inspiration for my name is Kang *Yuwei,* the reformer of 1898, whose name implies that he was going to do many great things; "*Yupuwei*" means, on the other hand, a man who refuses to do many great things. Of course, all opposites are essentially alike, and fundamentally Kang Yuwei and myself agree wonderfully well, although we talk so differently. For we have the authority of Mencius that it is the man who refuses to do many things that can do something.

Another merit of this name is that it suggests Chinese culture. It may suggest "I can't do anything," "I really haven't done anything worthy," "I am an utterly worthless fellow," and so on. It is therefore entirely in line with other equally cultured titles like the "Nursing Ignorance Studio," or "Ancient Stupidity Hut," or "Concealing Folly Mountain Shed" (which may be on the third floor of the Continental Emporium).

My friends have often asked me why I have called my study by that name and what are the great things that I have not done. It is a rather intriguing question, not only for me but also for everybody. It is a question that requires a great deal of heart searching. I hardly knew the number of things I had not done myself, until someone first asked me this question, and now I am sitting in front of my typewriter to think it out. I already have a feeling that I may require God's forgiveness for many of the things that I *have* done, but really my omissions are truly my great qualities that may land me in heaven after all. So, here they are:

I have never begged for a single autograph.

I have never been able to repeat Dr. Sun Yat-sen's will, nor have I been able to keep my mind from wandering during the official three minutes of silent worship.

I have never divorced my wife and am totally unqualified for being an educational leader.

I have never appeared in foreign dress as presiding officer in a meeting for the promotion of native goods, nor have I ever gone in a limousine to an athletic meet in order to encourage sport.

Nor have I ever thought anything of the people who do these silly things.

I have an abhorrence of physical effort, and have never sat on a fence; nor have I turned a somersault, physical, spiritual, or political. I can't even tell which way the wind blows.

I have never written a line that pleased the authorities or secured their admiration, nor have I been able to draft a single pronunciamento that has met with the approval of the great men.

Nor have I ever said anything that would please everybody; I haven't even tried to do so.

I have not called the moon square one day and called it round a week afterwards, for I have a very strong memory.

I have never seduced young girls and do not therefore consider them dangerous goods; nor do I think with long-legged Chang Chungchang that girls ought to be forbidden entrance to public parks in order to foster my private morality.

I have never taken a cent from the people of China without working for it.

I have always liked a revolution, but have never liked the revolutionists.

I have never been comfortable and smug and self-satisfied; I have never been able to look at my face in the mirror without a feeling of creeping shame.

I have never scolded or kicked my servants and let them consider me a great curiosity. My servants do not have any admiration for my money-making ability: they always know where my money comes from.

I have never suffered my servants to "squeeze" with legitimacy, for I don't give them that honest feeling that, by squeezing from me, they are helping to return the people's money to the people.

I have never sent articles to the papers about myself or let my secretaries do it for me.

I have never ordered good enlarged portraits and distributed them to my sons to be hanged in their respective parlors.

I have never pretended to like the people who dislike me. I have never been suave and polished and dishonest.

I have such a strong dislike of petty politicians that I have never been able to carry on a fight with them in any organization that I am connected with. I have always run away to avoid seeing them, for I don't like their faces.

I have never been cool and detached and unimpassioned and diplomatic in discussing my country's politics. I have never been scholarly and weak-kneed and hypocritical.

I have never patted a man on the shoulder and been philanthropic and been elected to a Rotary Club. I like the Rotary Club about as much as I like the Y.M.C.A.

I have never rescued any girls in the city or heathens in the country.

I have never been conscious of sin.

I think I am about as moral a man as anybody and that if God loves me half as much as my own mother, he will not send me to hell. If I don't go to heaven, the earth is doomed.

11

CRYING AT THE MOVIES

BECAUSE I often cry at movies, I always like a person sitting next to me silently blowing his or her nose or leaving the theater with a shining streak over his face. I am inclined to think that he is a better man for that. Now I honestly think crying at the movies is nothing to be ashamed of. It does one a lot of good. Let me explain what I mean.

"Did you cry?" my wife asked me, as we were coming out of the Nanking Theater after seeing Victor Hugo's *Les Misérables* on the screen.

"Of course I did," I said. "Any one who doesn't cry at

this great story which runs the gamut of our emotions isn't much of a man, is he?"

In fact, I was emotionally played out. I had a headache that evening, and just couldn't do anything. I tried to play poker, but it was a listless game, and I lost $4.25.

What is all this nonsense about not crying at a good story, whether it be on the screen or in a story book? In order to be respectable, let me show that I have Aristotle and Ssema Ch'ien on my side. Aristotle speaks of the true function of tragedy as a form of "catharsis," a purging of our emotions, and our greatest historian and prose writer speaks of it as "setting our blood in smooth circulation." If a great writer writes a great story which is played on the stage, and the audience does not cry, then something must be wrong with the actors or the audience.

It is disgraceful, it is unmanly to cry, you say. To a certain extent, this is true of everyday life. If a man cries or laughs too often, you say he is a sap, a sentimental and temperamentally unbalanced fellow, or an infantile idiot. All this is true, but isn't there a time when a man ought to be touched profoundly and shed a few tears? In a movie, life is presented to us in a more concentrated form, exciting our passions in a way that our everyday life can't. What, then, is all this talk about the cathartic functions of tragedy if it cannot even move us to tears—if it cannot move us who are so tamed and disciplined and conventionalized and proud of our conventionality?

Isadora Duncan once spoke of a woman as a musical instrument, and compared a woman who had only one lover to a musical instrument which had been played upon only by one artist. Every great lover makes a different sweetheart of the same woman, as every artist elicits from the same instrument a different music. Every work of art is a matter of response between the artist and the material or instrument of creation, and again between the artist and the reader or spectator, as the case may be. The same picture therefore may excite one man to ecstasies while it leaves another cold, whether it be a screen picture or a painting. The more sensitive the onlooker is, and the more finely responsive he is to the appeals of the work of art, the more he draws out of the picture, in comparison with others who are of a more phlegmatic temperament. The same sunset may excite one man to tears and be just an ordinary sun going down for another. The staid businessman who is proud that he does not grow sentimental over an ordinary sun going down—does he not cry sometimes, cry for joy when his stocks jump up 100 per cent in a day, or cry out of despair when the banks are closing his credit? What then is all this nonsense about not crying, and about crying being unmanly?

The fact is, some men are more sensitive than others, as there are good and bad violins. A great work of art requires a finely appreciative soul to draw from it the full enjoyment of which it is capable. The same thing is true of a good horse and a good jockey, and of a good musical composition and an understanding musician or conductor who can draw out of Schubert all the tenderness that is in Schubert, and out of Brahms and Tchaikowsky all the sorrow that is in Brahms and Tchaikowsky. And so it is true also of books and authors. Every man's appreciation of a good author is strictly limited by his own mental and emotional endowments. One man appreciates one line, another man appreciates another, and only rarely do we find a perfect sympathetic response between reader and author, as we find between a musical composition and a masterly interpretation by a gifted conductor.

Yes, there are tears in this life, and what matters after all is what we cry at. There are tears of delight and tears of sorrow, and tears of love and tears of forgiveness, tears of parting and tears of reunion between mother and child. Some cry at a mawkish sentimental story, while others cry at sheer beauty and kindness. But whoever feels like crying, let him cry, for we were animals before we became reasoning beings, and the shedding of a tear, whether of forgiveness or of pity or of sheer delight at beauty, will do him a lot of good.

12

MICKEY MOUSE

ONE of the most difficult things for me to put over to my Chinese-reading public is to convince them that humor is a part of life and therefore should not be shut out even from serious literature. This is as difficult as it has been for me to convince them that Confucius was a human being and always loved a good joke, even at his own expense.

It is perhaps difficult for a Westerner to realize the moral background against which an advocate of the proper role and dignity of humor has to fight. For according to the old tradition, no one except a clown would condescend to crack a joke in public, and Chinese editors and statesmen regard it as shocking and not permissible in good form to relieve their serious discourses on the salvation of the country with a touch of humor. There may be humor in a London *Times* editorial, but there may be no humor in a *Shun Pao* editorial. Many a young man, either in his middle school or just out of college, has charged me with ruining China by the introduction of humor. This is just like all juvenile thought and sophomoric wisdom in the West. But there are two special influences which seem to encourage the middle school student or the fresh college graduate in thinking this way. First, there is the tradition of the Sung philosophy, which was responsible for banning the novel and the drama from the field of Chinese "literature" proper, to the extent that practically all the great Chinese novels were written by anonymous writers. Second, there is the influence of the new school of "proletarian literature," which believes that literature should become a handmaid to politics and regards all literature which is not political propaganda as worthless. For this reason, I had to write the following essay on Mickey Mouse to correct my juvenile critics.

My middle-school critics who talk like men of forty would, of course, never consent to write on such a silly topic as Mickey Mouse. I am quite sure that they have even lost the capacity for enjoying a Mickey Mouse cartoon. So much the worse for China, if that is the case. For myself, the animated cartoons on the screen constitute one of the greatest blessings of mankind, being a form of art which transcends all limitations of time and space and gives full reign to human imagination in a way that is impossible in other forms of art. Just as the movie transcends the limitations of the legitimate stage by having at its disposal a freer command over scenery and a greater number of "extras" in the production of mass action, so the animated cartoons transcend the limitations of the camera. Magic carpets can fly easily in the air, storks can carry babies in bags and drop them down chimneys, a Mickey Mouse army can shoulder rifles and march into a fairy palace, pianos begin to shake their legs, clocks begin to cast wistful glances, and hot dogs begin to dance. There we are carried back into the dream world of our childhood in which nothing is impossible. The cartoons, therefore, achieve for us a liberation of the human spirit and transfer us into a magic world so long as that picture lasts. Now I know that my middle-school critics regard a Mickey Mouse cartoon as merely silly, but I have to remind them that when President Wilson was burdened with the heavy duties of the White House, his favorite relaxation was not to attend a Shakespearian play, nor to listen to Verdi's opera, but to forget himself in riotous laughter over cheap vaudeville shows.

I am far from saying that literature should be merely regarded as a form of relaxation. But I am strongly opposed to the proposition that only socialistic propaganda may be called literature. It seems to me the function of literature is to make us look at life more clearly, more correctly, and with a truer understanding and greater sympathy. Human life, however, is too complicated to be conveniently summed up by any one socialistic label or conveniently pigeon-holed into any one single doctrine. The view of literature which relegates it to the position of a handmaid of politics necessarily kills it by withholding from it the free play of the mind. Even political propaganda defeats its own purpose by constantly dilating upon the virtues of the political leader who subsidizes the paper. Literature must, in the first place, touch the human heart, and if only its picture of life is true, it cannot do any harm.

To my mind, the comic strips have brought more good to humanity than volumes of socialistic propaganda. I confess that I have been reading the comic strips for the last twenty years and have not yet ceased to derive a constant delight from them. "Dumb Dora" pleases us, and in pleasing us, it shows us the fickleness, light-heartedness, and the spirit of contradiction of the modern girl. "Mutt and Jeff," on the other hand, serves to remind us of something of the primitive manhood which modern civilization, or any civilization, is in danger of losing. I have no doubt that its influence on American boys is decidedly healthy. For if Mutt thinks nothing of falling thirty feet to the ground and getting a big lump on the forehead, there is no reason why Jim or Harry should be so afraid of his skin. Those two eternal adventurers would have died an untimely death long ago if they had a less tough constitution and their scalps and spinal columns were of a softer fiber. But there they are, still alive and full of fun, and ready for their hundredth adventure and hairbreadth escape from death. I cannot say exactly what socialistic doctrine it teaches, but I know it is good for the twentieth-century reader to be daily reminded that a fall from the housetop does not always mean instant death and that a bandage on one's face is not necessarily a disfiguring of one's countenance.

But above all, I should urge my "proletarian" critics to read carefully every morning "Bringing Up Father." They can regard it as a supreme satire on bourgeois snobbery in the person of Mrs. Jiggs and the best propaganda encouraging rebellion of the proletariat in the persons of Mr. Jiggs, Dinty Moore, and Company. I suggest this in all seriousness to my juvenile friends, even if they should have lost all capacity for enjoying that particular comic strip as mere fun. Between their heavy disquisitions on the methods of saving China, which is so much in need of salvation, let them take their minds off that topic for a while, and try to get a little smile, even if they have forgotten how to laugh, from the drawings of Mr. McManus. Let them read it with righteous proletariat indignation if they want to, but don't sneer at comic strips because they are comic strips. Shut your eyes to Mr. Jiggs's cigar, if you regard it as depraved bourgeois comfort, but at least learn humbly from these silly pictures a few lessons of the human heart—Mrs. Jiggs's snobbery in the first place, her fascination for aristocratic names, her false love of the opera, her slavery to fashion, the entire selfishness of her life, and, on the other hand, the sufferings of poor Mr. Jiggs, a good proletarian at heart, always relishing his corned beef and cabbage and pining for proletarian liberty among his gambling friends at Dinty Moore's, but unfortunately married into a false middle-class life.

All I can say is, if the young men of China have lost the ability for enjoying "Mutt and Jeff" and "Bringing Up Father," and a Mickey Mouse cartoon, then China is doomed. If proletarian literature is forced to take such an attitude to life, then proletarian literature is also doomed, for I believe with Confucius that anything inhuman cannot last.

13

BUYING BIRDS

I LOVE birds and hate dogs. In this, I am not queer; I am
merely Chinese. It just comes natural to me, as to all Chinese.
For the Chinese always have a weakness for birds, but when
you speak to them about kindness to dogs, they will just ask
you, "What do you mean?" I never could understand why
a man should befriend an animal and hug him and fondle
him. The only time I came to understand this feeling for
dogs was when reading the *Story of San Michele* by Axel

Munthe. The part where he tells of challenging a Frenchman to a duel on account of the latter's kicking a dog really moved me. It seemed then that I really understood him, and I almost half wished I had a faithful pointer to nestle by my side. But it was all the magic of his pen. That refined, luxurious feeling for dog friends was soon dead in my heart. The most annoying moment in my life was when, in the parlor of an American friend, a gigantic St. Bernard was trying to lick my hands and arms and be friendly, all made worse by my hostess trying to tell me of his pedigree. I must have looked like a heathen at that time, staring at her blankly and not able to find an appropriate word of approval.

"A Swiss friend of mine brought it straight from Zurich," said my hostess.

"Yes, Mrs. Pearce."

"His great grandfather on the maternal side saved a child from an Alpine avalanche, and his great uncle on the paternal side was the champion of an international dog show in 1856."

"Quite."

I didn't mean to be impolite, but I'm afraid I was.

I can understand that Englishmen love dogs. But then Englishmen love anything. They love even tomcats.

Once I argued this out with an English friend of mine.

"All this talk about befriending dogs is pure nonsense," I said. "You pretend that you love animals. You are a good liar because you send out these animals to hunt down a poor fox. Why don't you pet the fox, and call him my poor little innocent dear?"

"I think I can explain this to you," answered my friend.

"The dog, as an animal, is peculiarly human. He understands you, stands by you. . . ."

"Wait a minute," I said, interrupting him. "I hate dogs exactly because they are so human. I am naturally kind to animals, as is well proved by the fact that I cannot deliberately crush a fly. But I hate any animal that pretends to be your friend, that comes and paws all over you. I like animals that know their place, and keep their place. I prefer donkeys. . . . Be kind to a dog, yes, but why pet him and fondle him and hug him?"

"Oh, well," said my English friend, "I shan't try to convince you," and we switched over to other topics. Since then I have kept a dog, because the situation of my house requires it. I have him fed and washed properly, and he sleeps in a good kennel. But I have forbidden all his demonstrations of love and loyalty by pawing all over my body. Certainly I would rather die than lead him through the streets as so many fashionable ladies do their dogs. I once saw a Kiangpei *amah* with unbound feet on high-heeled shoes, evidently the servant of some English household, holding a cane in one hand and tugging at a terrier in the other. It was a sight, and I didn't want to cut such a ridiculous figure myself. Let the Englishmen do it. It goes with them, but not with me. When I go for a walk, I want to walk like a gentleman.

But I was going to speak about birds, in particular about my experience in buying birds one day. I had a large cage of small birds, I don't know of what name, but tinier than sparrows. The males have a red breast, with white spots on them. Several of them had died off the last winter through one accident or another and I had been thinking of buying a few more to keep the rest company. It was the Mid-Autumn Festival, and the whole family had gone out to a party, leaving me alone with my littlest girl. So I proposed to her that we should go to the Chinese city and buy some birds, and she agreed.

The bird street in the City Gods' Temple requires no description for any resident of Shanghai. It was a paradise for any true lover of animals, because there were not only birds, but also frogs, white mice, squirrels, crickets, tortoises with a kind of water plant growing on their backs, gold fish, sparrows, centipedes, lizards, and other monstrosities of nature. You should see the cricket sellers and the crowd of children surrounding them, and then decide whether the Chinese are lovers of animals or not. I went into one of those bird shops owned by Shantung people and, knowing the price for the variety I wanted, had no difficulty in buying three pairs. They cost me exactly two dollars and ten cents.

The shop was at a street corner. There were about forty of those little birds in a cage, and when we had settled about the price the man began to select three pairs for me. The flutter in the cage raised a cloud of dust about, and I stood aloof. By the time he was half through with getting those birds, a huge crowd had collected in front of the shop, natural perhaps for holiday-goers. The moment I paid my cash, however, and took the little cage away, I became the center of all attention and an object of popular envy. An irresponsible gaiety was in the air.

"What is that bird?" a middle-aged man asked me.

"You can ask the shop man," I said.

"Can they sing?" challenged another.

"How much did you pay for them?" asked a third.

I answered curtly, and walked away like an aristocrat.

For I was the proud possessor of birds among the Chinese crowd. There was something that bound the crowd together, a common delight, entirely natural and instinctive, that let loose our feeling of common brotherhood and broke down the barrier of reticence among strangers. Of course, they had the right to ask me about those birds, the same right that would entitle them to ask me questions if I had won the National State Lottery right before their eyes.

I then went along, with my child and my little bird cage. Everybody turned around. If I had been the child's mother, I should have chosen to believe that they were admiring my child, but, being a man, I knew they were admiring my birds. Are these birds so rare? I asked myself. No, they were just interested in birds as birds. I went up into a restaurant. It was early in the afternoon, and the top floor was empty.

"I want a bowl of *wonton*," I said.

"What are these birds?" asked the waiter, with a towel across his shoulder.

"I want a bowl of *wonton,* and a dish of white-cut chicken," I said.

"Yes, yes, do they sing?"

"Sing? Can the white-cut chicken sing?"

"Yes, yes, *one bowl wonton!—one dish white-cut chicken!*" he shouted, or rather sang, to the kitchen downstairs. "These are European birds."

"Is that so?" I asked just to be polite.

"They grow on the mountains, mountains, you know, big mountains. Hey, *changkwei,* what are these birds?"

The *changkwei* was a sort of account keeper. He wore a pair of spectacles, and as in the case of all account keepers, men who could read and could write, you wouldn't expect him to show an interest in children's toys, or in anything except dollars and cents. But the moment he heard there were birds, he not only answered, but, to my great surprise, moved his legs about to search for his slippers, left his counter, and walked slowly toward my table. When he came near the cage, his apathetic face melted, he became childish and garrulous, which did not go with his appearance. Then he pronounced his judgment, with his head raised toward the ceiling and his big belly projecting beyond his jackets.

"They don't sing," he remarked officiously. "Just cute-looking and good for children to look at."

And he went back to his high place on the counter, and in time I finished my *wonton*.

The same fate befell me on my way back. People bent over to catch a glimpse of what I had got. I went into a second-hand bookshop.

"Have you any Ming Dynasty editions?"

"What are those birds you've got there?" asked the middle-aged owner of the shop. The question turned the attention of the three or four customers in the shop to the cage in my hand. There was quite a flutter—outside the cage, I mean.

"Let me have a look," said a boy apprentice, and he snatched the cage from my hand.

"Take it and have a good look," I said. "Have you got any Ming editions?" But I was no more the object of attention, and was left free to mouse round by myself. Entirely unrewarded in my search, I took the cage and came out and became once more the center of attention. People smiled at the birds, or at me for possessing the birds.

Then I took a taxi at the corner of Szechuen Road and Avenue Edouard VII. It was at this spot, I remembered distinctly, that last time I brought back a cage from the City Gods' Temple, the man came out to look at my birds. This time he did not see them, and I was not interested in attracting his attention. But when I got into the car, the chauffeur's eyes caught sight of my little cage, and his face relaxed, and, sure as anything, he became childish, too, like the chauffeur on my last bird-buying trip. He was extremely friendly to me, our conversation got very far, and by the time I got home he had told me not only the secrets of keeping birds and teaching birds to sing but also all the secrets of the entire Ford Hire Service, the number of cars they possessed, the tips they got, the history of his entire childhood, and the reasons he disliked marriage.

I know now what to do in case I ever have to appear in public and try to silence an angered Chinese mob thirsting for my blood. I shall bring along a bird cage and show them a beautiful blue finch or a good singing skylark. It will be more effective than a fire hose or a tear-gas bomb, and it will win them over quicker than a speech of Demosthenes, and we'll all be friends.

14

MY LIBRARY

I PUBLISHED in *Jen Chien Shih* an article by Miss Yao Ying—she is really a Mrs., but she is not Mrs. Yao Ying, and in English there seems no way to refer to a lady's name without revealing whether she is married or not. There is the further nuisance of referring to a well-known woman writer and having to drop her first name the moment you introduce the word "Mrs." In China, at least, we can use the term *nu-ssu* without thus committing ourselves, in the same way that we can refer to a third person without distinguishing between "he" and "she"—a measure of sexual equality which obtains only in the land of Cathay. Couldn't we, I wonder, just address a person by a generic "M" and leave out of our curiosity whether it's a married or unmarried "he" or a married or unmarried "she"? Well, M. Yao Ying wrote a charming article on her way of arranging books in her library, which so coincided with mine that, had I ever published a word on the subject or ever seen her, I should have accused her of stealing my ideas. I therefore wrote a long editorial postscript to it—I wish editors would write long postscripts—showing how dangerously near her theory came to mine. In fact, we have only one common theory, which is roughly as follows: (translated from her article)

Of course, it's all right for public and college libraries to have a catalogue system, and have the books properly labeled and classified, either according to the Dewey or the Y. W. Wong system. But this is manifestly impossible with a poor scholar, who hasn't complete library editions to show off, and who often occupies a small terrace house in Shanghai or Nanking. This terrace house generally consists of a dining room, a parlor, two bedrooms, two bathrooms, and he is lucky if he or she has a study of his or her own [this grammatical nuisance exists only in the translation, and not in the original]. Besides, his or her small collection is generally of the personal sort, likely to be strong in his or her favorite authors and deficient in others. What, then, is he, or she, going to do about it?

I don't know about others, but this is my way [I am glad of this transition from the third to the first person, for the English language has unaccountably forgotten to distinguish a masculine and a feminine "I" and "my"]. My way is the natural way. For instance, when a book or magazine comes by post when I am sitting at a desk, then I leave it at the desk. If, in the midst of reading it, a visitor calls, then I bring it along to the parlor, and share it with my friend. When the friend is gone, if I forget to take it back, then I leave it in the parlor. But sometimes the conversation has been so interesting that I am not quite ready for sleep yet, but only want to relax a little; then I bring it upstairs and read it in bed. If the book can sustain my interest, then I read on, but if the interest slacks, then I can conveniently use it as pillow. This is what I call the natural way, which may be roughly defined as "the way of leaving books where they are." I can't even say there is any "favorite" place for my books.

The logical consequence of this system is, of course, that there are books and magazines all over the place, on the bed, on the sofa, in the dining room, in the sideboard, near the washstand in the lavatory, etc., giving thus a richness of impression unattainable by the Dewey or the Y. W. Wong system.

This system has three advantages to recommend it. First, there is beauty of irregularity. The books thus stand side by side, leather-bound editions, paper covers, Chinese, English, big heavy volumes, and light artistic copies, some with pictures of medieval heroes, others with nude modern girls, all mixed up in a wild profusion of learning, covering at a glance the whole course of human history. Second, there is richness and variety of interest. I let a volume on philosophy stand side by side with a treatise on natural science, and let a humorous booklet rub shoulders with some perfectly well-meaning moral-uplifters. They just form a motley company, pretending to hold diverse opinions with each other and get involved, in my fancy, in some hot mythological debate for my amusement. Third, this system has the advantage of obvious convenience. For if one were to put all the books in the library, one would, obviously, have nothing to read in the parlor. With this system I can always improve my mind even in the toilet.

Only I wish to say that this is merely my personal way, and I am not seeking for other people's approval, or asking them to follow my example. I am writing this merely because my visitors often shake their heads or heave a long sigh when they see the way I live. As I have not asked them, I do not know whether it is a sigh of disapproval or sigh of admiration. . . . But I don't care.

The foregoing may well serve as a good example of the familiar essay in China today. It has the lightness of touch of the old Chinese essay and the careless ease of the modern. The following is a brief translation of my long editorial postscript. I said:

When I received this manuscript, the title caught my attention as if somebody had stolen a great treasure from me, and when I read on, I discovered, to my great amazement, that my favorite theory on the collection and arrangement of books had been already discovered simultaneously by an independent worker. How can I therefore help saying something on the subject? I know that reading is a refined occupation, but since reading came under the control of college registrars, it has degenerated into a cheap, vulgar, mercantile business. The collection of books, too, used to be a refined pastime, but now things have sadly changed, since the *nouveaux riches* came in for this line of antiquarian business. These people always have complete works of this author and complete editions of that writer, bound in handsome morocco and so well kept in nice glass cases, which form part of their show to their friends. But when I look at their shelves, there are never any blank spaces or missing volumes, which fact shows they have never been touched except by their servant for the purpose of cleaning and dusting. There are no dog ears, no finger marks, no accidentally dropped cigarette ashes, no carefully blue-penciled emendations, and no maple leaves between the covers, but plenty of uncut pages.

So it seems even the collection of books has degenerated into a vulgar fashion also. Hsu Hsieh of the Ming dynasty wrote an article, "On Old Inkstones," exposing the whole vulgarity of collecting curios, and now Miss Yao has carried the idea forward to the collection of books, and my heart feels tickled. It seems if only you would say what you really think, there must always be others in the world who agree with you. The Y. W. Wong system is all very fine for public libraries, but what have they to do with a poor scholar's study? We must have a different principle, that pointed out by the author of *Fou-sheng-liu-chi,* namely, that of "showing the small in the big, showing the big in the small, meeting the real in the unreal and meeting the unreal in the real." The mentioned author was giving his private opinions on a poor scholar's house and garden arrangements, but the principle really holds good with regard to the arrangement of books. With the wise application of this principle, you can transform a poor scholar's library into a veritable unexplored continent. My theory is this:

Books should never be classified. To classify them is a science, but not to classify them is an art. Your five-foot book shelf should be a little universe in itself. This effect is achieved by letting a book of poems incline on a scientific paper, and allowing a detective story to keep company with a volume of Guyau. So arranged, the five-foot shelf becomes a *rich* shelf, intriguing your fancy. On the other hand, if the shelf is occupied by a set of Ssema Kuang's *Mirror of History,* then in moments when you do not feel inclined to look into the *Mirror of History,* the shelf can have no meaning for you, and it becomes a poor shelf, bare to the bones. Every one knows that women's charm lies in their mystery and elusiveness, and old cities like Paris and Vienna are so interesting because after staying there for ten years, you never quite know what may turn up in a narrow alley. The same thing is true of a library. There should be that mystery and elusiveness which comes from the fact that you are never quite sure what you have hidden on that particular shelf some months or years ago.

All books must have their individuality and must not have the same binding. That is why I never cared to buy the *Sse-pu-pei-yao* or *Sse-pu-ts'ung-k'an.* Their individuality partly comes from their appearance and partly from the circumstances of the purchase. You may have picked the volume up casually in a small town in Anhui while on a summer tour, or some one may have been trying to bid higher than you did for the volume. Now suppose the books have been bought and placed on a shelf in their natural way, and you have an occasion to look up Wang Kuowei's *History of Yuan Dramas,* a small, tiny volume. You start out as if on a hunt, and look for it on top and below, on the east and on the west, and when you have found it, you have really *found* it, and not just taken it. A few drops of perspiration are already formed on your brow and you feel as happy as a hunter on a lucky trip. Or perhaps, you have just tracked it down to its lair, and just as you are looking for the volume three you want, you discover it has disappeared again. You stand there, transfixed for a moment, wondering whom you have lent it to, and heave a great sigh of regret, like a schoolboy just missing a bird he nearly caught in his hand. In this way, a veil of mystery and charm will forever hang over your library, and you will never know what you are going to find. In short, your library will possess the elusiveness of women and the mystery of great cities.

Some years ago I met a fellow teacher in Tsing Hua, who had a "library," which consisted only of one case and a half of books, but which were properly labeled and classified, from one to one thousand, according to the American Library Association system. When I asked him about a history of economics, he could at once tell me, with great pride, that it was "580.73A." He was very proud of his American efficiency. He was a true American-returned student, and by that I mean no compliment, either.

15

CONFESSIONS OF A VEGETARIAN

THERE are vegetarians and vegetarians. Some are so by principle, others by temperament, and still others simply because they cannot digest a good beefsteak. The war among the vegetarians of various groups is greater than that between all of them and the non-vegetarian outsiders. The vegetarians by principle call the vegetarians by temperament half-hearted epicureans, while the latter regard the former as weak-hearted mollycoddles who shed tears at the sight of a dying chicken. The vegetarians by temperament also claim that the vegetarians by principle are no true vege-

99

tarians at all, that they do not know how to enjoy their vegetables, that they are slaves of their principle, and that, furthermore, they are merely frightened at the sight of a full-blooded beefsteak. Many vegetarian monks have confessed to me that they actually sicken at the smell of cooked meat. Needless to say, both of these groups have nothing but utter contempt for that class of consumers of sour milk, to which John D. belonged, who have strayed into the vegetarian camp by accident and on no greater merit than an outraged and now completely destroyed digestive organ. Toward a fourth group, the women heroically fighting their own waistline, who eat gingerly a mouse's slice of white chicken meat or nibble like rabbits at the outer crust of a pork pie, we vegetarians generally feel merely amused and take a kinder attitude.

You will have gathered that I am a vegetarian by temperament. The difference between a vegetarian by temperament and a vegetarian by principle is like that between a celibate monk and a married Protestant pastor. The former, I gather, is really afraid of women and so goes for total abstinence—at least, in theory. The Protestant pastor believes that he can marry a woman without at once giving up his soul to Mephistopheles, and that he can keep his sexual life within normal decent bounds without endangering his spirituality. That is a good, brave thing to do. It bespeaks faith in oneself and in human nature. So it is with a vegetarian by temperament. We think nothing of eating a steak, and God knows how I enjoy a steak!

Lest there be any misunderstanding, let me establish my position clearly. There is a philosophy behind it. I am a Chinese, and, as a Chinese, I do not believe in being a slave of any principle. No Chinese believes in going the whole hog in anything. This is the age-old doctrine of the Golden Mean. Be a lover of vegetarian food, yes, but why be logical about it? Be a good vegetarian, but don't be a thoroughgoing one. The aim of Chinese education is to cultivate a reasonable mind. A logical mind says, "If A is right, then B is wrong," but a reasonable mind always says, "A is right, but B is not wrong either." A reasonable reformer is not a new broom that will sweep the universe clean, but is always glad to leave some dirt behind. A reasonable teetotaler is an occasional wine-bibber; a reasonable antigambler is willing to play poker with five-cent stakes, and a reasonable vegetarian always relishes a roast Nanking duck or a blood-dripping beefsteak. As Confucius would have said, what boots it a man to have discovered the greatest scientific truth and be inhuman?

Now, there is a special point in being a vegetarian of the temperamental type. After munching six or seven duck gizzards, consuming one-fourth of a two-pound fish, one chicken drumstick, just a slice or two of fried mutton and onions, two or three shrimp balls, two spoonfuls of crab-meat, three spoonfuls of sharks' fins, and finally helping himself to a generous portion of roast duck, he sees a bowl of cabbage and chicken soup, waxes eloquent, and cries, "Ah! that cabbage is delicious! I am always for vegetable soup. All the chicken flavor has gone into the cabbage!" There is your perfect "vegetarian by temperament." He knows how oily the meats have been, and he always ends up by being a greater believer in cabbage cooked in chicken soup. Like an official who has loved the people and amassed a half-million-dollar private fortune, he feels how sordid the whole affair of politics has been, and now is ready to retire to the mountain forests and enjoy the autumn moon. He waxes eloquent over the autumn moon. Down in his heart, he has a deeper and more real appreciation of the purity and serenity of the autumn moon than a farmer who has seen the moon for the last fifty years of his life. He appreciates vegetarian food for the same reason that a prostitute appreciates the beauty and dignity of a home life. After that heavy dinner, he wakes up next morning and says he will have nothing to do with meat, takes a bowl of congee with salted carrots, falls to the temptation of a full-flavored brown cutlet at lunch, and ends up by being still more enthusiastic for vegetables that night when he goes to bed.

At this point, or long before that, the vegetarian by temperament and the vegetarian by principle part company. "What's the use of being a vegetarian and eating cabbage unless the cabbage is cooked in chicken soup and the chicken flavor has gone into the cabbage and the cabbage flavor has gone into the chicken?" the vegetarian by temperament asks. From this point, it is easy to see that China is the only place for vegetarians to live in. The Europeans fry their pork separately, boil their carrots separately, and then serve them together on the same plate! Imagine the stupidity or the absurdity of cooking bamboo shoots without pork! What would become of the bamboo shoots? Leave the pork alone if you wish at table, but at least you must cook bamboo shoots with it, so that it will lend them some of its flavor. For this reason, I believe, there are no vegetarians by temperament to be found in the whole of Europe. There can be only bigoted, narrow-minded, monkish vegetarians who are slaves of their own beliefs. All the Europeans know about vegetarian food is "eggs and spinach." For a Chinese vegetarian, eggs and spinach are a calamity. How can one really enjoy vegetarian food if one eats eggs and spinach?

I believe they eat with a sense of duty rather than with a sense of enthusiasm, which is of course as idiotic as all thoroughgoing, logical-minded vegetarians should be.

The Europeans are really a funny lot. Having lost, or never known, the art of cooking vegetables, and having fed themselves on real, unadulterated, logical vegetables, they then proceed to give a man a logical steak, and when a man is eating a steak, he sees nothing but a steak. He holds a fork heroically in one hand and a knife murderously in the other hand and tells himself that he is going to eat meat this time. Does any one ever see the absurdity of it all? Some hold their knives and forks downwards, but at times, when they stop for conversation, they turn their knives and forks upwards, facing the interlocutor, and I always imagine the interlocutor a little frightened and made ill at ease by that menacing attitude, especially when their views happen to contradict each other. Will the Europeans ever learn to use wooden chopsticks and allow us to see less metallic weapons at least while we are eating?

16

ON BEING NAKED

NUDISM has come to America, I am told. Let it come! I just fail to see what harm it can do. I have been a nudist all my life without my knowing it.

Now it should be clearly understood at the beginning that I am a *reasonable* nudist, as against the doctrinaire and fanatic nudists, as I always am a *reasonable* vegetarian as distinguished from the fanatic vegetarians. Like all Chinese, and following the old doctrine of the Golden Mean, I am all for nudism at certain hours and in certain circumstances, in the bathtub, for instance, but I am dead against going down Broadway in the native garb my mother gave me. I can honestly tell you that it is beautiful to feel naked in one's bath-

tub, and if the bathroom window looks out on nothing more
sin-conscious than a few passing sparrows and a peeping
branch, it is even downright delightful to throw it wide open
and let the skin come into contact with the keen, cool air.
Notice how it puckers at slight cold and fills out and becomes alive and oozes certain natural oils under the action of
the sun—it is extremely delightful to experience this feeling,
I say, when in one's bathroom. It is decidedly radioactive—
I have no ghost of an idea what this word means, but I
know what it should mean—the action of the sunlight on
my skin. All sane and unbiased people should admit that
stripping and exposing oneself to the sun, say, for fifteen
minutes every day in a room protected from draft and neighbors' eyes, is, I affirm again, a most healthy and energy-giv-
ing experience. These people should hasten to call themselves the real, sensible, and reasonable nudists with me.

At certain hours and under certain circumstances, I say.
There is evidently a justifiable distinction between true
nudism and exhibitionism, as there is a true distinction between prayer on a mountain peak alone by oneself to one's
Creator and an exhibitionist prayer at one of those religious
revivalist meetings, which is a sermon preached to God for
the benefit of one's fellow revivalists. The one enjoys nudism
for its own sake and his own enjoyment, the other flouts
nudism in others' eyes and transforms his own naked body
into a billboard, saying, "Look here! I dare!" There are any
number of aspects of life in which this distinction holds: the
distinction, for instance, between loving one's wife or husband at home and calling him or her "darling" in public;
or between a realization of one's own shortcomings in one's
private chamber and confessing a childhood theft ten years
ago at an Oxford group meeting (omitting of course the

five-thousand-dollar crooked deal); giving a twenty-cent piece to a pretty beggar girl in a back alley at twilight and making an opening speech at a charity ball; horseback riding for one's own enjoyment and horseback riding with a diamond ring on one's finger and jade earrings on one's ears behind a painted face very nearly resembling stage make-up. All these things, I mean, are actually being done. One class include the genuine religious men, the loving wives, the charitable persons, and the true horseback riders, and the other—the exhibitionists.

In other words, I am a genuine nudist because I love to be naked when alone. I need not go into all the advantages, first among which is the realization that one is in the first place an animal, a sheer animal. Listen, if you can, at your own heartbeat, and watch, if you can, the blood coursing through your veins, and you'll get a truer mystic realization of the purpose of human life than from volumes of philosophy. A good, whole-hearted acceptance of the fact that we have a body, that so much depends on our body, and that we should take good care of this wonderful self-repairing machine of ours. Then being naked gives one a certain freedom of movement which is always lost when the least amount of clothing hinders its sway and flow of movement. Watch how delightfully free your knee is at bending when naked, as compared with bending it with trousers on. One might also practice a certain amount of running about in one's private room completely naked and enjoy that sense of absolute freedom, but I should take care that my servant does not see me at it. One has to submit to a certain amount of artificiality in life and be reasonable about it. If one's skin is sufficiently healthy, one will enjoy also sleeping naked, as all Manchus do for economic reasons, and enjoy the free contact between one's skin and the fresh, clean bed clothes. On the whole, all doctors will tell you, the skin is one of the primary organs for disposal of waste and an automatic antiseptic organism, and if one should, owing to the stupidity and inhumanity of Western clothes, be forced to enclose it cruelly in a tight-fitting underwear, preventing or interfering with all its natural excretory action, one should at least allow a few minutes in the twenty-four hours every day for it to resume its natural function in its natural state, particularly under the influence of the sun and fresh air. Aesthetically, too, I think, it helps to make one conscious of the rhythm of one's movements.

But aesthetically, if for no other reason, I am dead set against exposing one's body in public. Artists know, if poets don't, how rare a perfect human form is. A beauty may have a gorgeous torso, but disgracefully weak calves and disproportionate feet. Any one who persists in believing that the average human body is beautiful to look at should just go to any beach on a summer afternoon and take a look at nature. Any one with sensitive eyes will run away in horror. Susan, who is thirteen, is too skinny; Betty has too many lumps round the hips; Uncle George does not look nice naked with his spectacles on and his head bald; sister Kate is too flabby round the chest, while Aunt Cordelia is a downright fright. In the whole family, I see only Julia is divine. As the Chinese say in describing a beauty, add a tenth of an inch and she is too plump; take away a tenth of an inch and she is too thin. She is just right. But how many persons in this universe are just right? And how many of them remain just right after they are past their prime?

Consistent nudism, therefore, is only endurable in a society of men and women blind to their own ugliness, and if carried to its logical end, would mean a general atrophy of our aesthetic sense. There will be then about as much aesthetic appreciation of the body beautiful as among the naked aborigines of an African jungle. The average human body looks either like a monkey or an overfed horse, and only clothes help some to look like colonels and others like bank presidents. Strip them and farewell to the colonels and the bank presidents! Their occasional nudism at home explains why they are generally thought beneath contempt by their wives. Strip the high and mighty delegates to international conferences naked, and we would have gained a truer insight into the present world chaos, being essentially ruled by monkeys.

I am sure that, in a world where nudism has become conventionally respectable, almost all women will long for a rag to cover up the persistent forgetfulness of their Maker. After all, the downfall of man and the coquetry of woman began with a fig leaf. Just think how many women in the nudist world will improve their figures by wearing a brassière, and how many more by wearing a corset! Those who have the audacity and the shameless immorality to use these feminine contrivances will then be denounced by the older and more respectable women for not leaving their breasts exposed. "Those shameless modern ladies are not playing fair!" Mrs. Grundy-in-the-Nudist-Republic will exclaim. "Why, the younger Miss Strachey even wears a rag over a foot long round her hips. I don't want to spread rumors, and haven't seen it with my very own eyes, but so they say!"

"Well, there's nothing that these modern young wenches will stop at nowadays," replies Mrs. Dundee. "I shouldn't be surprised if some day they should extend this rag round their hips even to conceal their knees. You know these young ones, they dare anything to shock the public."

And then men will fall in love merely with a brassière, or die for the sight of a long petticoat.

So I say, if nudism comes, let it come! It can do no harm. I have full confidence that our human sense of the beautiful has not all gone to the dogs and will act as a natural deterrent against excesses.

I am usually not interested in people's morals, but this seems the most decent thing I ever wrote.

17

HOW I MOVED INTO A FLAT

ONCE I moved into an apartment flat. If an American had heard it, he would probably have said, "Oh yeah? Is that a fact!" If an Englishman had heard it, he would probably have said, "Oh, dear, what a fall!" But being a Chinese, I simply said to myself, "Can do, it's my fate."

I was forced into it. I didn't want to move, that is, not exactly, if my neighbor would have stopped that radio of his. Now, ordinarily, if a neighbor peers into your house, you can close your window shutters. Against people's inquisitive eyes, you may even build a high stone wall in front, and transform your home into a fortified castle, ready to defy the whole world. You can also stop the telephone with a rag when you do not want to be disturbed. But against ubiquitous house-breaking radio music you are defenseless. I was at my neighbor's mercy, since he had decided to buy a radio set and let me share it gratis. He could exalt me or depress me, let me hear Strauss or Stravinsky or Mei Lanfang just as he wished, and for as long as he thought fit. He was especially fond of Jeanette MacDonald's "March of the Grenadiers" and of Soochow crooning, which is a species of asthmatic delirium. I always listened whenever he wanted me to, but I finally got tired of it. It's all right to listen to Mozart or Mendelssohn when you are tinkering or repairing the toilet, but not when you are thinking how to pay your tailor's bills, or how to write a biting reply to an anonymous letter and make sure that it reaches the nasty gentleman. And when it comes to Soochow crooning, the asthmatically delirious style is apt to get into your writing.

Under such circumstances, an Englishman would go to his neighbor and say, "You stop that, or I shall write to the police." A Chinese gentleman with any culture at all would prepare to adapt himself to the environment and seek the peace of his soul by ignoring the existence of his nerves. Being an English-educated Chinese, I could do neither. So when, for the fiftieth time, I heard Jeanette MacDonald singing, I wrote a "To Let" notice and posted it on my house. I had to go—anywhere.

To live in an apartment is against my nature. I still insist that I shall think nothing of modern civilization until it can make it possible for every man to have a few yards of soil which he can call his own, where he can plant peas and tomatoes, and where his children can catch crickets and get comfortably dirty. I have said that I don't believe in the combination of buttons, switches, cabinets, rubber mats, keyholes, wires, and burglar alarms which they call a "home" in modern civilization. I always laugh in my sleeve when some modern salesman tries to impress upon me the modernity and convenience of a hybrid thing which is a sofa in daytime and a bed in the night. I always tell him I am unimpressed. A sofa should be just a sofa, and a bed a bed. The convertible sofa-bed is to me a symbol of the mutilation of the modern home and of the very important fact that modern civilization is cheating man of his proper place in the sun. The modern spiritual home is broken up because the modern physical home is cramped and visibly disappearing, on account of such abominations as apartment flats, aided and abetted by motor cars. People move into a three-room flat and then wonder why the younger generation never stays at home. At least, if we have to sleep on a bed which is the back of a sofa seat in the day, let's not be proud of it. Even a mouse generally manages to have more space for his sleeping quarters.

But I moved into an apartment flat in spite of my inherent prejudice against it. It was the old trees that did it. Unbelievable as it may sound, there was actually an apartment in Shanghai which looked out on some undisinfected grand old trees growing amidst a wilderness of underbrush and green meadows. As the temptation was difficult to resist, I yielded.

I did not have to keep pot flowers. My study window looked out on a mass of green foliage, whose reflected mellow greenness suffused the whole room. And I did not have to keep a bird cage. Not that I don't love birds. Like Cheng Panchiao, the only true bird lover in the world, I hate to see birds in cages. In his letter to his younger brother, the poet says that the only proper way to love birds is to live near a forest, where one can see from one's study window golden orioles jumping from branch to branch and red-breasted pheasants trailing clouds of glory as they dart from tree to tree, or where one can overhear the love song of cuckoos when one least expects it. As I was writing in my flat, birds were darting across my window and two or three sparrows were having their love chatter some twelve feet from my desk. When I was lucky, some of them came and perched on my window sill, persuaded that creatures like us are not all Ku Klux Klan hundred per cent blond beasts. If I had stayed long enough, I believe I might have been able to learn the bird language. If I were a poet I could write a stanza in their honor, in true Chinese fashion:

> Green, green,
> The Sterculia leaves.
> Blue, blue,
> The sky behind them.
> Light, light,
> The early autumn breeze.
> Gone, gone,
> My heart's sorrow burden.
> Chirp, chirp,
> The birds' love chatter.
> Gay, gay,
> Their autumnal dress.
> Now, the feathered lover flies away,
> Because his bride disdains his attentions
> When a new one perches by her side.
> But I still look on,
> While I am thinking of the one gone away.

18

HOW I CELEBRATED NEW YEAR'S EVE

THE old Chinese New Year, of the lunar calendar, was the greatest festival in the year for the Chinese people, compared with which every other festival seemed lacking in completeness of the holiday spirit. For five days the entire nation dressed in its best clothes, shut up shop, loafed, gambled, beat gongs, let off firecrackers, paid calls, and attended theatrical performances. It was the great day of good luck, when everybody looked forward to a better and more prosperous new year, when everybody had the pleasure of adding one year to his age and was ready with an auspicious luckbringing word for his neighbors.

The humblest maid had the right not to be scolded on

New Year's Day, and strangest of all, even the hard-working women of China loafed and ate melon seeds and refused to wash or cook a regular meal or even handle the kitchen knife. The justification for this idleness was that to chop meat on New Year's Day was to chop off good luck, and to pour water down the sink was to pour away good luck, and to wash anything was to wash away good luck. Red scrolls were pasted on every door containing the words: Luck, Happiness, Peace, Prosperity, Spring. For it was the festival of the return of spring, of life and growth and prosperity.

And all around, in the home courtyards and in the streets, there was the sound of firecrackers, and the smell of sulphur was in the air. Fathers lost their dignity, grandfathers were more amiable than ever, and children blew whistles and wore masks and played with clay dolls. Country women, dressed in their best, would go three or four miles to a neighboring village to watch a theatrical show, and village dandies indulged in what flirtations they dared. It was the day of emancipation for women, emancipation from the drudgery of cooking and washing, and if the men were hungry, they could fry *nienkao,* or make a bowl of noodles with prepared sauce, or go to the kitchen and steal cold cuts of chicken.

The National Government of China has officially abolished the lunar New Year, but the lunar New Year is still with us, and refuses to be abolished.

I am ultra-modern. No one can accuse me of being conservative. I am not only for the Gregorian calendar, but am even for the thirteen-month calendar, in which all months have exactly four weeks or twenty-eight days. In other words, I am very scientific in my viewpoint and very logical in my reasoning. It was this scientific pride which was badly wounded when I found my celebration of the official New

Year a great failure, as anyone who pretended to celebrate it with any real feeling must have found out for himself.

I didn't want the Old New Year. But the Old New Year came. It came on February the fourth.

My big Scientific Mind told me not to keep the Old New Year, and I promised him I wouldn't. "I'm not going to let you down," I said, with more good will than self-confidence. For I heard rumblings of the Old New Year's coming as far back as the beginning of January, when one morning I was given for breakfast a bowl of *lapacho,* or congee with lotus-seeds and dragon-eyes, which sharply reminded me it was the eighth day of the twelfth moon. A week after that, my servant came to borrow his extra month's pay, which was his due on the New Year's Eve. He got an afternoon's leave and showed me the package of new blue cloth which he was going to send to his wife. On February first and February second, I had to give tips to the postman, the milkman, the expressman, the errand boys of book companies, etc. I felt all along what was coming.

February the third came. Still I said to myself, "I'm not going to keep the Old New Year." That morning, my wife told me to change my underwear. I said, "What for?"

"Chouma is going to wash your underwear today. She is not going to wash tomorrow, nor the day after tomorrow, nor the day after the day after tomorrow." Being human, I could not refuse.

That was the beginning of my downfall. After breakfast, my family was going to the bank, for there was a mild sort of bank panic, which came in spite of the fact that by ministerial orders the Old New Year didn't exist. "Y.T.," my wife said, "we are going to hire a car. You might come along and have a haircut." I didn't care for the haircut, but the car was a great temptation. I never liked monkeying about a bank, but I liked a car. I thought I could profitably go to the City Gods' Temple and see what I could get for the children. I knew there must be lanterns at this season, and I did want my youngest child to see what a rotating lantern was like.

I should not have gone to the City God's Temple in the first place. Once there at this time of the year, you know what would happen. I found on my way home that I had not only rotating lanterns and rabbit lanterns and several packages of Chinese toys with me, but some twigs of plum blossoms, besides. After coming home I found that someone from my native place had presented me with a pot of narcissus, the narcissus which made my native place nationally famous, and which used to bloom so beautifully and gave out such subtle fragrance on New Year's Day in my childhood. I could not shut my eyes without the entire picture of my childhood coming back to me. Whenever I smelt the narcissus, my thoughts went back to the red scrolls, the New Year's Eve feast, the firecrackers, the red candles and the Fukien oranges and the early morning calls and that black satin gown which I was allowed to wear once every year.

At lunch, the smell of the narcissus made me think of one kind of Fukien rice pudding, made with turnips.

"This year, no one has sent us any turnip pudding," I said sadly.

"It's because no one came from Amoy. Otherwise, they would have sent it," said my wife.

"I remember once I bought exactly the same kind of pudding in a Cantonese shop on Wuchang Road. I think I can still find it."

"No, you can't," challenged my wife.

"Of course I can," I took up the challenge.

By three o'clock in the afternoon I was already in a bus on my way home from North Szechuen Road with a big basket of *nienkao* weighing two pounds and a half.

At five, we ate the fried *nienkao,* and with the room filled with the subtle fragrance of narcissus, I felt terribly like a sinner. "I'm not going to celebrate the New Year's Eve," I said resolutely; "I'm going to see the movies tonight."

"How can you?" asked my wife. "We have invited Mr. Ts—— to dinner this evening." It all looked pretty bad.

At half past five, my youngest child appeared in her new red dress.

"Who put on the new dress for her?" I rebuked, visibly shaken, but still gallant.

"Huangma did," was the reply.

By six o'clock, I found red candles burning brightly on the mantelpiece, their lapping flames casting a satirical glow of triumph at my Scientific Consciousness. My Scientific Consciousness was, by the way, already very vague and low and unreal.

"Who lighted the candles?" again I challenged.

"Chouma did," was the reply.

"Who bought the candles?" I demanded.

"Why, you bought them yourself this morning."

"Oh, did I?" It cannot have been my Scientific Consciousness that did it. It must have been the Other Consciousness.

I thought I must have looked a little ridiculous, the ridiculousness coming less from the recollection of what I did in the morning than from the conflict of my head and my heart at that moment. I was soon startled out of this mental conflict by the "bomb-bah!" of firecrackers in my neighborhood. One by one, those sounds sunk into my deep consciousness. They have a way of shaking the Chinese heart that no

European knows. The challenge of my neighbor on the east was soon taken up by my neighbor on the west, until it grew into a regular fusillade.

I was not going to be beaten by them. Pulling out a dollar bill, I said to my boy:

"Ah-ching, take this and buy me some heaven-and-earth firecrackers and some whip firecrackers, as loud as possible and as big as possible. Remember, the bigger and the louder the better."

So amidst the "bomb-bah" of firecrackers, I sat down to the New Year's Eve dinner. And I felt very happy in spite of myself.

19

AH FONG, MY HOUSEBOY

MY HOUSEBOY was a real "boy," not only in the colonial, but also in the physiological sense of the word. He was just a kid, but an unusually brilliant kid. When I picked him up at a small exchange shop where I used to change my money, he was but fifteen, or at most sixteen. When he was eighteen, his voice had so changed that it reminded me of a young rooster that has just learned to crow in the morning. But in spirit he still remained a kid, and his kiddish spirit, plus his brilliance, formed a combination which made all discipline impossible in the household, and successfully baffled all my attempts at establishing a master's dignity.

He was so brilliantly good that he was almost indispensable, but he was about the most delightfully chaotic, poetically forgetful, and charmingly unbusinesslike servant I ever had, and he broke more bowls, cups, and tumblers in a week than all my other servants did in six months. And yet he was lionized in the kitchen, and compelled something like involuntary admiration from us for his genius. Perhaps it was because of the realization that he was too good a fellow creature for a servant. I have no doubt he would have made a splendid master, judging by the way he scolded midnight callers over the telephone. He did not read English, but who can tell but some day he may (so many things about him have surprised me), so we will call him Ah Fong because this isn't his name.

I have to explain just why I allowed Ah Fong to break down the moral discipline of the household and do many things that I would not stand for from other servants. Before he came, the job of repairing electric bells or burned-up fuses, adjusting mechanisms in the flush toilet, or seeing to the proper way of hanging a picture used to fall on my hands. After he came I simply let him do it, and I could go on with my reading of Plato's *Republic* without being called upon to fix the flush toilet, and do my writing without somebody shouting to me from the kitchen: "Hey, the water tap is leaking!" That feeling of security alone was worth all the troubles I suffered at Ah Fong's hands. He was a genius in providing unthought-of and happy makeshifts for all sorts of mechanical devices, and for thinking up fairy tales to keep my children in the garden.

There was an incident which endeared him to me. Ever since the first day he came, he had his eye on my typewriter. He pretended to take two hours to clean my study every day in the morning while I was still in bed, whereas I knew he was peering into and monkeying with this marvelous writing machine, which he evidently had seen for the first time in his life. Strange sounds used to come from the study at such hours. Then one day the typewriter went out of commission. I spent two hours repairing it, but failed. I scolded him for monkeying with it. He did not reply. But in the afternoon I was out, and when I came back, he told me quietly, "Master, the machine is repaired." After that, I respected him as a human brother.

In many other ways he was indispensable. He would answer telephone calls and scold the callers in English, Mandarin, Shanghai, Anhwei, and Amoy dialects, this last being a language which few outsiders ever have the courage to learn or the luck to succeed in learning. How he picked up the English phrases and sprung them upon me as a surprise with such perfect accent was a secret between himself and his Maker. He said "waiterminit" and not the "wai-t-a-me-enyoo-t" of the Chinese college students. I tried to persuade him to take up night school studies and offered to pay two-thirds of his tuition, but he wouldn't. I know he did not like school.

This partly explains the reason for my tolerance. But what service I got from him! I would send him to a shop round the corner to get a tin of metal polish, and he would disappear for an hour and come back with a pair of new shoes for himself and a grasshopper for my children, but no metal polish. Happily he was not gifted with a sense of distinction between work and play. It took him three hours to clean the bedroom, because he would stop in the middle of the work and take an hour off pretending to clean the bird cage, or would run down to frisk and frolic with the new washing maid. "Ah Fong, you are eighteen now, be serious about your work," my wife would say. But what was the use? He broke my dishes, burned my brand-new table knives in the oven, dropped pans on the floor, left the dustpan and the floor cleaner in the middle of the drawing room, while he was off hunting for grasshoppers. There was hardly a set in our china closet left complete. And what a noise he made in the kitchen, when he was hurrying for my breakfast—"bing! . . . bang! . . . splash!" He had taken over the duty of preparing the breakfast from the cook's hands because, I suspect, he liked the job of frying eggs. And the cook allowed him.

The cook, by the way, was a widow of twenty-six, as stupid and homely-looking a creature as you could find anywhere. There is something about the tenderness and devotion of such stupid creatures that is often touching. I can still remember the tone in which she always spoke Ah Fong's name. One summer night I woke up at midnight from the oppressive heat, and heard whispers in his room. He had just come in from the yard and the cook had followed him there! They were whispering! I was all ears. But there followed—only dead silence. She had gone in to make the bed for him. It was just a touch of maternal kindness.

Then came a new washing maid and what a change in the life of the kitchen! The new maid was twenty-one, jolly, vivacious, and she liked Ah Fong, too. A continuous banter of words and laughter went on in the kitchen now. Work became more slipshod than ever; the noise of laughter grew louder. Ah Fong became more forgetful of his work. Cleaning one room took longer and longer hours. Ah Fong began to forget even to polish my shoes in the morning. I told him once, twice, three times, with no effect. Finally I threatened to sack him, if the next morning my shoes were not polished and placed before my bedroom door by half past six. I grouched and thundered the whole day, and did not talk with him. I intended to restore the moral discipline of the household. The master's words must be obeyed. Before retiring that night I repeated the threat of discharge before the boy, the cook, and the new washing maid. All looked scared, the cook and the new maid more than the boy. I was sure now that I would be obeyed.

The next morning, I woke up at six and waited patiently to see the effect of my order. At twenty past six, the new maid brought up the shoes instead of the boy. I felt cheated out of my rights.

"I wanted Ah Fong to bring them himself. Why do you do this?" I asked.

"Oh, I was coming upstairs, and I thought I would bring them along with me," answered the maid, sweetly and politely.

"Why couldn't he bring them? Did he ask you to bring them or did you offer yourself?"

"No, no, he did not ask me. I offered, myself."

I knew she was lying. Ah Fong was still in bed. But her tactful defense of Ah Fong somehow touched my heart. So I willingly let my discipline be broken down, and let the case drop. Thereafter I was not supposed to know what was going on in the kitchen.

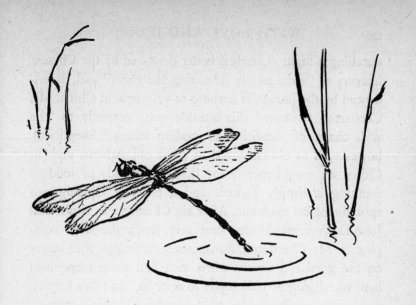

20

CONVICTIONS

MR. G. K. CHESTERTON once lamented that the art of newspaper controversy had decayed with the decay of "strong convictions of faith" in modern days. That, Mr. Chesterton thought, was "the principal line of cleavage between the new journalism and the old. What emerges now in most discussions on political, philosophical, or religious problems is seldom a definite argument at all, but a sort of detached nature study—as if the writer were watching and describing the flight of birds."

He was mistaken in considering this lack of strong convictions a modern malady. The cool, detached way of treating truths which he compared to that of a naturalist watching a flight of birds is better described by the Chinese imagery of "a dragon-fly skimming the water" and, as evidenced by the phrase, is nothing so very new in China. Mr. Chesterton attributed this attitude quite correctly to "the wide chasm of skepticism in modern society." Skepticism, however, is as old-fashioned as good old Athens, and, in China, we would merely say that this malady of modern thinking is simply Taoistic and a form of Chuangtsean epistemological epidemic. After all, Chuangtsean truths and John-Deweyesque truths wear very much the same complexion. Mr. Chesterton, for instance, ruminated with regret on the good old times "when men had some recognized basis of religion or philosophy to refer to," and "an Imperialist might justly exclaim to the Socialist 'I think your attempt to blow up the King is highly un-Christian,' and the Socialist could retort, 'I consider that your policy of annihilating the Niggers is abominable.' " Had Chuangtse been born as late as 1905, and had he been present at such a verbal controversy of the Imperialist and the Socialist, he would have laughed at the "strong convictions of faith" of these moral gentlemen until his sides split and his contorted face looked like one big question mark.

I am not here to defend skepticism, modern or ancient, but to describe a mental malady which is clearly my own. This malady has gone so far that it often put me in a most embarrassing and disadvantageous position on many social occasions. I remember, while at college, during the outbreak of the European War, how I envied the moral convictions of my schoolmates who were able to say, with impressive certainty, that the war was all brought about by the Germans, who alone should be held responsible. Later on, after Russia left the Allies and went on a unique socio-political experi-

ment known as the Bolshevist Revolution, I was still more
impressed by the schoolmates, and even by some of the
teachers, who were able to form clear and decided opinions
on the wicked Bolsheviks. I knew that if I ever should be
able to arrive at such clear and decided opinions about the
Bolsheviks, it would be after an arduous and tortuous process
of long thinking, beset all the way by doubts and hesitancies,
while these fortunate gentlemen were able to arrive at the
same result by a brilliant flash of genius, as it were. These
gentlemen did not argue with me. When I offered my
doubts, they simply answered me with an annihilating look,
or laughed me out of court.

My embarrassments are by no means confined to such
academic discussions on social or political topics. Not only
professors and college students squashed me by their overpowering convictions, but even commercial salesmen have
done so. The tones of both classes are so much alike that it
is difficult to say who should have received greater com-
mendation from Mr. Chesterton. Only the other day I was
buying a Remington typewriter for my office. I didn't particularly mean to buy a Remington. To me, an Underwood
would have been just as good. I was not able for my life to
tell the difference in excellence between an Underwood and
a Remington. In short, I had no moral convictions on the matter. It was a pure accident that I sent for a Remington agent,
and not for that of Underwood. But, to my surprise, I was
told there was a world of difference between a Remington
and an Underwood: the latter, for instance, didn't have a
semicircle of soft springs which protected the striking keys.
Why, there was no comparison between the two, he said,
and he thought I should be well informed enough to know
that "Big business brains prefer Remingtons." I frankly told

him that I didn't have big business brains, and was not likely to have any, now that I was already past thirty-five. He told me, on the sly, that some years ago one of the big typewriter companies was so poorly managed that it nearly went bankrupt. This left me in a worse confounded state of mind than before, and I saved myself by quietly buying his machine.

The choice of cigarettes offers another example of my mental malady. Now, I have fairly sensitive nerves and I am a fairly heavy smoker, always believing in cigars or a pipe rather than cigarettes. People therefore cannot accuse me of lacking a connoisseur's "flair" for taste in tobacco. But, up to the present time, I have never been able to say which make is the best. I have successively experimented with Capstan, Gold Flake, Fatima, Westminster, Three Castles, and Craven "A." But I have never been able to say, with any modicum of moral conviction, which make is the best. I have always liked Capstan, because it is invariable, but the moral righteousness of Capstan men got on my nerves. I consistently maintain that the perfect enjoyment of Lady Nicotine depends as much on the smoker's state of nerves as on the tobacco itself, and there are times when I enjoy a Ruby Queen at 20 coppers a packet as much as I do Capstan at five times that price. I am a moral coward, a renegade, an opportunist, as far as smoking is concerned. I have no fixed convictions on the matter. I may disown a Chesterfield today, knowing full well that some evening next week, when I am feeling my best, I may be offered Chesterfields and suddenly find that "they satisfy." I will take a Camel, when I have no other brand, but I will not "walk a mile for a Camel."

Why multiply instances? From the highest philosophical problems to the lowest questions of dealing with the kitchen maid, I am a prey to the same Chuangtsean epistemology.

Only the other day, a lady friend brushed me contemptuously aside, when I cast doubt on the idea that hospital servants should be tipped and nurses should not, stated with such cocksureness that it seemed she had reason, convention, and respectability all on her side. I envied her clarity of thought and expression. And didn't the Professor of Economics assure me that, in his opinion, there was no doubt that Dr. Sun was a greater economic philosopher than Karl Marx, in so energetic a manner and so close to my face that I felt the need of his gargling with Listerine or some other deodorant?

21

DO BEDBUGS EXIST IN CHINA?

BEING a gentleman, I have no opinions to give on any subject like this. But I am familiar with the rich variety of opinions and attitudes which different people represent, from Ku Hungming, Hu Shih, Chang Chungtsang, to the White Evangelist, the Buddhist-Taoist, the die-hard, and the *tangpu,* regarding such a question. All their different opinions are very interesting and worth studying. Bacon once wrote about the "idols of the tribe," "the cave," "the market," and "the theater," and we shall find all these idols of the human mind rather curiously and profusely illustrated in the diversity of opinions on this vexing topic.

Suppose we simplify the matter a little, and imagine that, in a distinguished gathering of Chinese and foreign friends at the home of a Chinese hostess, a bedbug chooses to make its social debut by crawling slowly but conspicuously across the specklessly white sofa cover. This is a thing that might conceivably happen in any household, English, French, Russian, or Chinese, but let us suppose it is Chinese. A patriotic Chinese gentleman who can talk very good English first discovers it, and his patriotism urges him to go and sit on the bug, taking all the chances of either killing it by his bodily weight, or, what is more likely, being bitten by it secretly for the sake of the honor of his country. To the consternation of all present and the extreme embarrassment of the hostess, however, another appears, followed by still another, until we have the unchallengeable fact that bugs exist in some Chinese households in some Chinese cities. We might hear therefore a Modern Symposium on the bedbug in China, which could be summarized by the following positions:

Attitude 1. "*Bugs exist in China, true; but that is the best proof of our spirituality. Only spiritual people are oblivious of their physical surroundings!*" The propounder of this brazen lie is no other than Ku Hungming. One can only condemn it as a brazen, though brilliant, lie, because by implication one would have to assume with Ku Hungming that the modern man using a sanitary flush toilet is less "spiritual" than one using the Scotch toilet.

Attitude 2. "*Bugs exist in China, true; but what of it? Bugs exist in Vienna, Prague, New York, and London, also. In fact, some of these cities are quite famous for it. It's no disgrace at all.*" This is the attitude of the Chinese "patriots," the "Orientalists," the "Pan-Asiatics" and the people who want to preserve our "national heritage" for us. General Chang Tsungchang was once so happy in discovering a bedbug at Unzen in Japan that he never stopped telling people of the consequent superiority of Chinese culture.

Attitude 3. "Bugs exist in Columbia University also. Hence the Chinese would be highly uncivilized not to have bugs in their beds. Moreover, the American bug has a better figure than the Chinese bug. So let's catch one, especially the California variety, import it to China, and put it on the Chinese bed." This is the position taken by the Columbia Ph.D. who cannot talk a word of Chinese.

Attitude 4. "What! Bugs exist in China? Bugs don't exist in England. Hence, I demanded extra-territoriality." This is represented by the die-hard. His first sentence is a truth, his second a lie, and his third the wittiest remark of the English daily editor, which never fails to secure applause among the Shanghailanders. It would not be at all surprising if the English daily some day published this with the glaring head-line, "TORTURED BY BEDBUGS: LIFE MADE A BURDEN FOR FOREIGN VICTIM OF CHINESE JUSTICE," should a foreign convict in a Chinese prison after the return of extra-territoriality give an account of his experience in a Chinese prison, with the amazing discovery that there are bedbugs in Chinese prisons.

Attitude 5. "What? Nonsense! There are no bugs in China, nor ever were any. They are the aberrations of your own fancy. I tell you there are no bugs in China." This is the position of the national propagandists, and the Chinese diplomats. Some eminent Chinese personage was responsible for the statement at the League of Nations that China had stopped cultivating opium around 1920. He was of course merely prosecuting his profession, and nobody can blame him. What else did the British and French delegates to the League of Nations do?

Attitude 6. "Let's not talk about it. And let's impeach the fellow who has the audacity to do so. He is unpatriotic," says the *tangpu* man. *"Serve him a warning,"* says another of his colleagues.

Attitude 7. "Don't disturb my contemplations. So long as I can remain happy while bitten by the bugs, what's the harm?" says the Chinese Buddhist-Taoist poet. To which Bertrand Russell gives a sympathetic half-nod. Didn't Cheng Panch'iao, one of the greatest literary lights of the Manchu Dynasty, sing once about the mosquitoes and the bugs?

Attitude 8. "Let's catch them," says Dr. Hu Shih, *"and see if there aren't more of them."* To which all the foreign Liberal Cosmopolitans would echo, *"Yes, let's catch them, no matter where they are and of what nationality they are."*

Finally, the last attitude, *Attitude 9,* is represented by the Little Critic. On seeing a bug making its social debut in a distinguished gathering, it is his habit to exclaim, *"Look, here's a big bug! How big and beautiful and well-fed he looks! How nice and ingenious of him to turn up at the psychological moment and provide some topic for our dull conversation! Was it your blood he sucked last night, my dear charming hostess? Let's catch it. There is tremendous fun in catching and crushing a big bug."*

To which my charming hostess could at best reply, "My dear Dr. Lin, you ought to be ashamed of yourself."

22

FUNERAL NOTICES

"ARE you popular, Mr. Lin?" once a great, big American-returned friend asked me. Any one can see that only a great, big American-returned friend can ask such a question. Having received some sort of American education myself, I did not reply in the negative. "Why, yes, certainly, considering the number of funeral notices and letters soliciting contributions I receive every month. I had no idea I was so well-known until last month when I received a funeral notice from somebody I did not know from Kwei-chow, followed by another from Szechuen."

Now, I am a very bad correspondent. All my friends will testify that my typewriter does not click for messages of good will and remembrance to the best and oldest friends. There are many ways of killing correspondence, and my favorite way is to keep them on the file for "Letters to be answered" until your conscience tells you that there is really no point in answering that particular one *now*—and down it goes to your right-hand drawer where you keep all your old correspondence safe under lock and key. And yet, with the best of precautions, it seems no one is safe from funeral notices nowadays. Of course, there are other things which are just as provoking, such as one of those chain letters from one of your most esteemed friends, promising you good luck if you copy them nine times and continue the chain started by some U. S. Colonel, but threatening you with bad luck on the ninth day, if you break it. I have received such chain letters from the most respectable quarters—one even from that citadel of Chinese learning, the Central University. Who on earth in that learned institution should have the audacity of threatening me with bad luck behind his initials is one of life's mysteries that I don't try to solve. The chain usually ends in a waste-paper basket so far as I am concerned.

Funeral notices are one of the finest fruits of this civilization of ours. They are the best proof in China that many of those who died have not died in vain, if they are survived by somebody who can write a good funeral notice. Not only does the career of the deceased receive thereby an immortal record, but those of his living sons and relatives get a chance of detailed description and enumeration also, i.e., those who send you the funeral notice without regard for a four-cent stamp. A man who dies not only with such an illustrious career, but also with the several illustrious careers of so many illustrious relatives, cannot fail to make you feel that life is worth living in China, and death worth dying, also. Any one who reads through the following sample of the last funeral notice I received will readily understand why a funeral notice is one of the things one actually lives for and looks forward to in one's old age. It runs as follows (for full effect, imagine that Mrs. Jiggs stands by while we read):——

"The unfilial sons undersigned, by neglecting to destroy themselves, have brought disaster upon their illustrious deceased father. The said deceased *fu-chun* was—a second-rank official of the former Manchu Dynasty, once a secretary of the Ministry of Finance, Tupan of Hwai Conservancy, Imperial Educational Inspector of the Two Kwang Provinces, Courier of the Imperial Southern Study, with Special Privilege of Wearing Flowery Plumes. *(Mrs. Jiggs, I am sure, is feeling exhilarated.)* . . . His brother was a Hanlin scholar and Tutor before His Imperial Presence, with the Special Honour of Drinking Wine with, and Receiving a Poem, from His Majesty. *(Mrs. Jiggs is inspired.)* This brother married the daughter of the Governor of the Two Hu Provinces, So-and-So, who was a Cabinet Scholar, once a Vice-Minister of the Ministry of Army, with the Special Privilege of Wearing the Yellow Jacket, Posthumous Title Loyal-Determined. *(Mrs. Jiggs' head is getting dizzy.)* . . . His eldest son is a Chin-shih of the year *chia-tz,* Taotai of Li-cheng, Examiner of the Shantung Province, and married the daughter of an Official of the Fourth Rank, the

Taotai of Hweichow. *(Mrs. Jiggs falls into a swoon; hence unaware of what follows hereafter.)* His second son is a graduate of the Military Academy of Paoting, Quartermaster of the Kansu Army, went abroad on a tour of Industrial Inspection through the countries of the United States, England, Germany, Denmark, Belgium, France, Italy, Austria-Hungary, and is now the President of the S—— Exchange Bank, decorated the Order of the Literary Tiger. His third son is a graduate of Cornell University; studied in the Harvard Post-Graduate Summer School; A.M. from Wisconsin, and Ph.D. from Columbia; Chairman of the Shantung Educational Association; Delegate to the nth Industrial Conference at Tokyo in 1909; served on the Board of Directors of the P—— University; Dean of the Political Science Department of S—— University; Vice-Chairman of the Society for Promoting Confucianism; Delegate to the Educational Conference at Peking, 1913; and now President of the Tsung-chih University; Order of Auspicious Corn. The fourth son is . . ." But it is time to sprinkle water on Mrs. Jiggs' head. All one can do is to gasp for breath.

It is not difficult to understand my popularity in receiving funeral notices now. If I were to base an estimate of my popularity on the funeral notices I have received, I can safely be said to enjoy a national reputation.

But it is also easy to understand why such funeral notices exercise such a powerful influence on high politics in the Orient. It is, for instance, a universally accepted fact that dear, old Tsao Kun bribed his way into Presidency of the Chinese Republic for no other reason than the anticipated pleasure of having the three characters *Ta Tsung Tung* incorporated in his funeral notice. It is equally certain that Chang Tsolin was tantalizingly seduced by the same idea of making himself the President of the Chinese Republic, shortly before the end of his regime in Peking, also from the same motive. One is not so sure but that Yen Hsishan was a victim of the same psychology in starting the Northern Rebellion. It would be difficult to account for it from any other standpoint so far as his personal interest is concerned. Had this custom prevailed on Mount Olympus, Zeus himself would not be satisfied with his blessed state and his occasional love affairs, but would raise a rebellion in high heaven until he added to himself the title of the Primeval Spirit of the Sea and Earth, and re-established his abode on the Himalayas and his summer garden on the Andes. It would read so much better on his funeral notice.

Such are the motives of the gods who guide and determine our human affairs. It seems after all the most difficult thing in this country is to die like a gentleman.

23

I COMMITTED A MURDER

I COMMITTED a murder after one of the most beautiful and exasperating conversations in my life. What with Christmas celebrations, fooling with the children, some indulgence in shopping, a little extra laziness consonant with the spirit of the holiday, I was late with my *Little Critic* article. Being otherwise a methodical man, I did feel, however, a little inclined toward being less methodical at this time. Could a man not forget his duties at this time of the year? Would the world go to pieces if the magazine failed to appear on December the 29th? Could I not fool around with the children a little longer and sit by the Arcola dreaming about a fireside and annihilate time for a day or so? However, my always strong sense of duty urged me to take a few worried looks at the typewriter. Like a Confucian gentleman, I harnessed myself for the work.

It was at this juncture, when one felt one had to write something and did not know exactly what to write about, that the bell rang. The servant presented a card. It was a stranger; that was the worst of it, for if he were an old friend, I could wish him Merry Christmas and tell him to go to hell. But evidently there was something very urgent about the call. I asked the servant to inform the gentleman that I was very busy, but that I should be willing to spare a few minutes, if the gentleman felt the business was very important. He said it was, and was shown in.

He was a well-dressed gentleman. There was something refined about him. One might have guessed it from his name card, which was in Sung Dynasty script. He had a beautiful forehead, suggestive of thought and scholarship, but a rather compromising receding chin, and his eyes were rather too small to be socially attractive. He carried with him a parcel. I hated him.

The conversation began. The gentleman had heard of my "great name." He had even read many of my books.

"They are entirely worthless," I felt obliged to say, according to the Chinese standard of courtesy. The moment I uttered these words, I felt a very strong misgiving. Instinctively I felt we were about to bandy compliments for a quarter of an hour before touching on the business on which he came. What on earth did he want?

Now I have had many conversations with these gentlemen. Invariably, the more educated my interlocutor was, the longer we had to bandy about compliments and beat about the bush. For the Chinese conversation with a stranger of the educated class is an art. There are rules about such a formal call. The conversation should have not only style, but also "composition," in the technical sense of the word. A perfectly conducted conversation runs from the beginning to the end like a Beethoven symphony. It has four movements. Unlike a Beethoven symphony, however, the theme or the

real business, does not come in the first movement, but at
the end. Briefly, the four movements are: (1) Meteorology,
(2) History, (3) Politics, and (4) what the fellow really
wants. No educated man would plunge into the fourth
movement, without discursive, introductory airs and varia-
tions. And the more discursive these preparatory airs are,
the abler the conversationalist proves himself to be. The first
movement merely prepares one's mind; it warms up your
feelings as it were. To this movement belong the *Compliments,* the *Weather Situation,* and the other *Meteorological
Aspects.* After one's mind has been thus properly warmed
up, there comes the second movement, which consists of
Reminiscences; you have met the gentleman before somewhere, or there might be some common friend, which sort
of intensifies your liking for each other. If he is from Peita
(Peking National University) and you are also from Peita,
then of course it is easy enough to pass in review the various
professors and call them by their first names, which shows
you are in the inner circle. The third movement consists of
Comments on Current Politics. Into this very wide field
fall: the necessity of saving China, the hopelessness of this
or that political leader, the latest civil war, episodes of Dr.
Sun Yat-sen, in which connection one could also bring in
any relation he had with the great leader. As far as my
experience goes, there is not one man of forty in China
today who does not have something to recount about that
great man on suitable occasions. At last, when you feel the
greater part of the useful morning has been mercilessly
murdered, the gentleman sips his tea, rises, is about to take
his hat, and springs the fourth movement upon you, which
is usually very short, and begins and ends like this: "By the
way, there is little thing I forgot to mention. You know per-

haps the President of the —— College. If you could write a letter of introduction to him for me, etc."

I felt on this occasion I was going to undergo these four movements of the symphonic poem this morning. There was a certain luxurious ease and largeness of movement about the way he opened his conversation that made me aware of what to expect. What did he hide in that parcel? My natural good manners prevented me from asking him also what the hell did he want. Or was he going to give me a job? Nevertheless, we began with Meteorology, as usual. This movement happened to be *Largo*.

When I thought we had counted all the stars in heaven, the gentleman happened to mention Mr. Fu, an old graduate of Peita, and now a very forceful writer. He was at the reminiscences, the second movement, now. Yes, wasn't he a fine boy? Marvelous force in his writing. I fully agreed. But my eyes were divided between my typewriter and his parcel. Still, in spite of myself, I did feel warmed up. The *Andante* about Mr. Fu was well executed. The comments were sound and sensible.

The passing from the second movement to the third movement was executed with great skill. Mr. Fu came from Szechuen. Szechuen was a very unfortunate province, the gentleman observed, because he had read somewhere in the *Analects Fortnightly* (a very subtle compliment to myself) that there had been 477 major and minor civil wars in that province since the establishment of the Republic. I could not but admire the justness of his observation, but was thinking in my mind, "Doesn't one have plenty of time in China?" The *Critic* boy was coming for my manuscript at eleven. I must help this gentleman through his third movement, for I was in no mood for beauty of movement. We had been talking for well over half an hour now, and I felt it quite safe to come to real business.

"Does Mr. S—— have some special business this morning?" The change of key was rather sudden, but it was well taken. "There is a little thing I want to consult you about," he plunged in, unwrapping his parcel. "I have heard that you are an old schoolmate of the editor of the F. E. Monthly. I shall be much obliged if you will pass this manuscript to him, and see if by any chance he could use it?"

"I do not know the editor and have not heard of the Monthly," I said, feeling like Macbeth committing a foul murder.

It was really a dramatic ending. He was less prepared for it than myself. Both of us felt like wanting to cry, but did not know how. For down in our hearts, there was a feeling of deep regret, that a conversation so well prepared for and led up to with such great trouble should after all be a material failure. Both of us felt the futility of human life— for I knew that I had wasted the best part of my morning, while he felt he had wasted so much of his meteorological, historical, and political wisdom.

24

A TRIP TO ANHWEI

IT IS difficult to write about travel, when one is suffering from a heavy cold. No one, I believe, ever comes back from a trip without being physically the worse for it. The good life is the regular life. School children are generally listless on Monday mornings, and teachers find their attention wandering after the Easter recess. Everybody brags about his week-end trip. He is bragging because his nerves are so shattered that he cannot concentrate his mind on a single topic. His nerves are a mass of weird sensations, memories of the dust and commotion on the road, mixed with recollections of parched lips and a parched throat, cool mountain breezes, beautiful moonlight nights, pale-faced monks, and silvery-voiced country maidens, all woven together as disorderly and illogically as in a dream. To this day, and after a long night of twelve hours' sleep, my nerves still tingle with these sensations and impressions. But that sleep was wonderful, the most wonderful I had ever had for years. No one realizes how beautiful it is to travel until he comes home and rests his head on his old, familiar pillow. I would give anything to have that sleep again. It is evidently worth all the physical ruination of your body that you incur by traveling away from home.

It was all like a dream, beautifully disordered like a dream. One was hurtled through space from winding motor roads on steep hillsides to peaceful pastoral landscapes. Hour by hour, the scenery changed kaleidoscopically. By and by, one got used to these novel changes, and began to doze off, and then one was awakened by a good friend's shout, "Oh, that wonderful peak!" Or, if it wasn't a wonderful peak, then it was a magically beautiful farmer's hut, with the door shut, and a peach tree blossoming in careless glory, dreaming its hours away in fragrant loneliness. My friend who was a poet immediately composed a beautiful poem on it. I still remember the last two lines:

The farmer's family has gone out to the field,
And the peach tree is weary of its loneliness.

But I am translating the untranslatable.

All this was on the newly opened motor road leading from Hangchow to Huichow (Hsihsien) in Anhwei. [I was supposed to write this article as a matter of publicity in return for the courtesy of the Chekiang Government in arranging for this beautiful motor trip free. But actually I wrote it to excite the envy of those who were forced to remain in Shanghai during the spring vacation, and make them curse themselves for not being able to get away.]

Of this trip, three things easily stand out in my memory as most worthy of the reader's envy. First, of course, is the emerald natural swimming pool along the motor road a few miles from Tangchiatun. All that section of the road from Tangchiatun to the other side of the Yulingkwan, or the mountain pass separating Chekiang from Anhwei, is scenically the most beautiful part of the journey. But that emerald pool easily tops them all. In fact, there are three such pools all by the roadside, about five feet deep and from one hundred to two hundred yards long. The water is of emerald color, and you could see every little pebble at the bottom. The bed of one of these pools is just one big piece of smooth-faced rock. How delightful, I thought, it must be to tour this spot on a summer afternoon and stand with your bare feet on this rock bed, and how beautiful it must be to see young women swimming in this clear, transparent pool, with the white, graceful rhythm of their bodies weaving into the green shadows of the mountain pines. It is truly idyllic, and near by is an idyllically situated village, called Sanyangk'eng, with hills all around and a babbling brook in the center of the valley, comparable to Switzerland itself. If any summer resort hotel is to be built, it should be built here.

Next to these pools, I should mention the pine forests and bamboo groves of Tienmushan, reached by three hours' sedan chair from Tsaoch'i station, which is two and a half hours by motor from Hangchow. The Shanyuanshi temple is situated at the foot of the hill. It is more a monastery than a temple, with accommodations of over five hundred beds for the annual pilgrims. Of these, there are about twenty first-class beds with excellent provisions for guests. The monks' vegetarian food is excellent and near by the living rooms is a mountain brook, with a series of cascades flowing over huge boulders. Yuan Chunglang wrote in the sixteenth century that at night his friend mistook the noise of these cascades for rainfall which, his friend thought, would spoil the next day's trip. To this day, that rainfall-like noise is ready to nurse to peaceful sleep any traveler who cares to go there. Directly behind the temple and all over the western Tienmu mountain, are gorgeous bamboo forests and tall pine trees, from a hundred to a hundred-fifty feet high. It is good to wander in these forests and lie on the ground and listen to the babbling brook and just do nothing.

Lastly, I should mention Tunch'i, which is the chief trading center in southern Anhwei. It is locally known as the "little Shanghai," and is connected with Hsihsien by an atrocious motor road—about an hour's ride. But the visit to the city is worth the discomforts of the drive. We slept on big, clean houseboats, and enjoyed the river scenery to the full. Layer after layer of hilltops line the horizon all around, while a broad river about a hundred feet across winds its way through the valley. A walk along the banks of this river on a spring afternoon can turn anybody into a poet. It is in a place like this that, according to the Chinese tradition, great beauties and poets are born, and I was half inclined to believe it. Some of my friends thought they saw some great beauties there. But I put it down to the magic of the place, which quite excusably upsets their balance of judgment.

25

SPRING IN MY GARDEN

I HAD come back from the trip to Anhwei to find spring
in my garden. Her steps had lightly tripped over the lawn,
her fingers had caressed the hedgerows, and her breath had
touched the willow branches and the young peach trees.
Therefore, although I had not seen her coming, I knew she
was here. The rose bugs, of the same green as the stem on
which they thrive, were again in evidence; earthworms
again put in their appearance by throwing up little clusters
of mud in the garden beds; and even those poplar branches
that I had chopped up into little pieces one or two feet long
and that were lying in a heap in the yard, performed a
miracle by putting forth green and merry leaves. Now after

three weeks, I could already see the shadows of leaves dancing on the ground on a sunny day, a sight that I hadn't seen for a long time.

What is happening to the animals, human animals and animal animals, is a different story. There is sadness all round. Perhaps it isn't sadness, but I have no other word for it. Spring makes you sad and spring makes you sleepy. It shouldn't, I know, and if I were a peasant boy, or if everyone in my household from master to cook had only to look after buffalos, I am sure we wouldn't feel sad about it. But we are in the cities, and cities make you sad. I think I have found the word now: it is called "spring fever."

Everyone is having a spring fever, including Chubby, my dog. I had cured my spring fever by taking a trip to Anhwei and seeing those emerald pools near Yulingkwan. But I had boasted of my trip before my cook, and he happened to be from Anhwei and it made him extremely sad. For he is washing dishes and cutting carrots and cleaning kitchen utensils in spring, and that makes him sad. My boy, a tall husky farmer from Kiangpei, is polishing windows and mopping the floor and sticking letters in the letter box and pouring out tea the whole day for me, and that makes *him* sad.

Then we have the cook's wife in our household as wash woman. I like her extremely because she is a very humble creature, fairly good-looking, and has all the virtues of a good Chinese girl; she keeps her mouth shut the whole day and works the whole day, moving about on her little half-emancipated feet, ironing and ironing and ironing and not saying a word, and she does not giggle but laughs in a natural quiet way when she laughs, and talks in a low voice when she talks. Perhaps she alone isn't feeling sad, for she is grateful that we have spring in the garden already, and there is so much green and so many leaves and so many trees and such a good breeze. She is grateful and she is satisfied. But what about it? It is all unfair. Her husband used to get her pay and gamble with it, and once even struck her until my wife stopped it by threatening to dismiss him if he did that again, in spite of the fact that he could make the best vegetable soup in the world. He will never take her out, so she stays in the house the whole year round. Then, finally, there is Huangma, *de facto* household manager and governess of my children, whose job is to see that everything is in its place and to put my gowns in the wardrobe the moment her eyes spot them lying about on a bed or an armchair in the fantastic fashion that I left them. With her, the world is so orderly that spring couldn't make any difference. She is past forty-five, I think, so she has seen forty-five springs in her life and she can't get excited over it. Not that I don't entertain the highest respect for these two women servants, for both of them have the best traditional Chinese breeding. Neither of them is greedy, neither of them is garrulous; both of them have their hair brushed in a neat fashion, both of them rise early to attend to household matters, and both of them are fit to bring up my children, if necessary.

But I was talking about the spring fever. The cook, a handsome dandy, is growing impatient of his work and giving us worse food than usual. He is listless most of the time, and makes his wife wash all the dishes in order that he may go out early. Then A-ching, the "boy"—he is really a tall man—came one day to me and said that he wanted leave for an afternoon. A leave for A-ching! I was completely surprised. I had told him to take a day off every month, but he had never done so. And now he wanted a half-day's leave to "arrange an important matter with a friend from his native district." So *he,* too, has caught the spring fever. I said, "Very well, but don't go and arrange the important matter with your friend from the country; go to the New World or the Great World, or take a sampan and just sit there, if you can't paddle, and look at the water." I grinned roguishly and he thought me a very sagacious and profound master.

While A-ching was taking leave from my home, somebody else was taking leave from office to visit my garden. It was the messenger boy from the K—— Book Company. He hadn't appeared for a long time, for a grown-up man had delivered the manuscripts and proofs and letters in the last month or so. Now the boy must take his place and come to my house and deliver the proofs, or perhaps a single letter, or a copy of a magazine, or even to convey me a good wish. That boy—I know he is living down in the eastern district, where you can see only walls and walls and back doors and refuse cans and cement floors, with not a green leaf around. Yes, green leaves can grow from the crevices of rocks, but can *not* grow from the cracks of cement floors. So he must come to my house every day or every other day, and must linger round, very much longer than necessary. For at least there is spring in my garden. Of course, he is not taking a spring outing. He is only bicycling to the western district to deliver Mr. Lin Yutang an important letter.

There is sadness, too, among the animals, by which I mean the real animals. Chubby has been a monk, and so long as spring isn't here, he is a contented dog. I always thought my garden big enough for him to play about, so I never let him out, for I derive no particular joy in taking a country walk if I have to tug at Chubby, and Chubby goes so fast that I have to tug hard to keep pace with him. But now the garden isn't big enough for him, not by a long shot, in spite of all the bones and the delicious left-overs. Of course, it isn't that. I understand him. He wants *her,* no matter blonde or brunette, pretty or ugly, so long as she is a she. But what can I do? I am perfectly helpless in this matter, and Chubby is very sad.

Then a tragedy happened to our little household of pigeons. There is really only a couple. There were six or seven of them, when I took over the house, but all left and only this sweet couple remained. They had tried to raise a family in the loft of my garage, but always had no luck. Two or three times a young pigeon was hatched and then it would learn to fly before it could walk and fall dead. I didn't like that look in the parents' eyes, twinkling and twinkling, and they standing silently round the opposite roof to contemplate the funeral. The last time, however, it looked as if they were going to be successful, for the young one was growing bigger every day, and had even come out to the loft window and gazed at the outside world and could already flap its wings. But one day, our whole household was thrown into a flurry by the announcement by the ricksha boy that the young pigeon was dead. How had he died? The ricksha boy had seen him just roll on the ground and die. It called for a Sherlock Holmes brain like mine.

Wonderingly, I felt over the body of the dead young pigeon. The pouch under the neck, which used to be full of food, was evidently empty. Two eggs were lying in the nest. The mother pigeon had been hatching again.

"Have you seen the father pigeon lately?" I opened the investigation.

"Not for a few days already," said the ricksha boy.

"When did you see him last?"

"Last Wednesday."

"Hm-hm!" I said.

"Have you seen the mother about?" I asked again.

"She didn't leave the nest much."

"Hm-hm!" I said.

It was evident there had been desertion. The spring fever had done it. It was death from starvation beyond the shadow of a doubt. The mother pigeon could not leave the nest, and she could not find food for the young fellow.

"Like all husbands," I muttered.

Now with her husband deserting her, and her young one dead, the mother pigeon would not even sit on the eggs. The family had been broken up. Sitting for a while at the opposite roof corner, and taking a last look at her former happy home (where her two eggs still lay), she flew away—I don't know where. Perhaps she will never trust a male pigeon again.

26

FREEDOM OF SPEECH

I WAS asked some years ago to speak to the China League for Civil Rights on freedom of speech. It is a great topic, and I was going to make my speech as free as possible. But this can never be done, for when anyone announces that he is going to speak his mind freely, everyone is frightened. This shows that there is no such thing as true freedom of speech. No one can afford to let his neighbors know what he is thinking about them. Society can exist only on the basis that there is some amount of polished lying and that no one says exactly what he thinks.

All this trouble comes from having speech at all. Only human beings have articulate language, for the cries of animals serve only as the signals for immediate instinctive needs, like the cries of pain, hunger, fear, and satisfaction. However varied the cries of a dog may be, they do not depart from his immediate emotional needs. When a tiger devours a man, he may groan with satisfaction, but he does not say like one of our pre-war generals when murdering a journalist, "Look here, my moral indignation compels me to devour you because you are endangering the safety of the Chinese Republic." Only mankind is capable of this truly human language. This is the difference between man and animals.

I agree therefore entirely with General Ho Chien, who once condemned modern school books for making Teddy Bear say this and Br'er Rabbit say that, thus accusing animals of things which they cannot say and making the animals appear as crooked as human beings. All Æsop's Fables are libels on the animal kingdom and would not have a chance of being understood by the animals if they could read them. When a fox fails to reach a hanging bunch of grapes, he just goes away: he is not such a bad sport as to call them "sour grapes." No animal except man can descend to such a low level. If a fox wants to force the Chinese farmers to plant opium by collecting opium taxes from the non-opium-growers he does not call them "Tax Against Laziness." Or if he did, he would not be an honest fox. . . .

You see, therefore, that the difference between man and animals is that man talks, while the animals at most squeal. Bernard Shaw has rightly said that the only kind of liberty worth having is the liberty of the oppressed to squeal when hurt and the liberty to remove the conditions which hurt them. The kind of liberty we need in China is exactly this liberty to squeal when hurt, and not the liberty to talk. All of us talk enough, but few of us dare to squeal when hurt. Our language is so refined that it seldom expresses our vital needs. That, to my mind, is also one of the differences between man and animals. When a cat starts howling at night, he generally has all the freedom he wants, and his howling is always expressive. Not so the Chinese farmer. When he is hurt, he goes home to curse, and is afraid to make his curse audible.

This liberty of speech is a foreign notion, for there has been no such thing in China. With our great common sense, we have always praised silence rather than speech. As one of our sayings goes, "All diseases come in through the mouth, as all troubles go out from the mouth." Chinese officials have always been careful to "dam the people's mouths more than they dam the river." And the people's mouths are always dammed. The only saying I have been able to find which authorizes some kind of freedom of speech is the following:

Let them laugh and scold who want to laugh and scold.
A good official am I, a good official am I.

But this does not mean exactly the same thing as freedom of speech. For only when the people's laughter and scorn do not hurt, do they have that freedom. When they hurt, the "good official" may shoot them.

We must realize, therefore, that all speech is a nuisance and that the liberty of speech is still a greater nuisance in the eyes of officials. Officials like quiet people who do not talk and who do not squeal when hurt. For instance, if there was a detective of the Public Safety Bureau present at any speech, I am sure he was thinking me a great nuisance, while he thought all of the audience who sat there so quietly and "kept their mouths shut like vases" better citizens than myself. This lies in the nature of things.

We must realize that the liberty of speech we demand for the people means that there is going to be no liberty of action for the officials. The officials love their liberty as much as we love ours. When we demand liberty of the press, we are really demanding that the officials' liberty to muzzle the press be taken away from them. When we demand liberty of person as a constitutional right, we are taking away from the officials their liberty to chop off people's heads. The two kinds of liberties are diametrically opposed to each other. It cannot be helped.

If I were an official, I, too, would love to have the liberty of chopping people's heads off on a sour morning, as many as I like and whenever I like it. I know that General Chang Yi of Changchow, my home town, had this liberty and enjoyed it. Whenever he felt depressed and could find nothing exciting to do to relieve his mental depression, he would just write two lines on a slip and order some prisoners to be beheaded in his presence, to cure his headache. I can safely report this fact, because General Chang Yi is dead.

Therefore when the China League for Civil Rights came in to curtail the officials' liberties and champion the people's civil rights, the League became a great nuisance in the eyes of the militarists and the officials. The militarists would have liked to condemn people to death in secret tribunals, but the League demanded open trials. The officials would have liked to kidnap their opponents and make them disappear from the surface of the earth, but the League wanted to send public telegrams, demanding to know their whereabouts. The League promised to become a greater and greater nuisance in proportion as it was able to carry out its program.

This is nothing new in Chinese history. When the Tunglin scholars at the end of the Ming Dynasty stood for free and fearless criticism of the government, they were compared to the 108 robbers in the romance of *Shui-hu*. Their names were publicly banned. They died at the hands of eunuchs. In their place rose people headed by Ts'ui Ch'enghsiu, a group which their contemporaries characterized as consisting of "five tigers, five leopards, five dogs, ten sons, and forty grandsons." Nevertheless, the Tunglin scholars were imprisoned, tortured, and beheaded, while the tigers and leopards and dogs won.

It would be foolish to expect that the present situation will be different. Anybody who wants to champion the people's right of speech must have eunuchs for his enemies. The difference between the China League for Civil Rights and the Tunglin scholars of Ming Dynasty is that the League was fighting for the principle of free speech *as a constitutional principle*. When the Tunglin scholars impeached the notorious eunuch and traitor Wei Chunghsien, all that the infamous eunuch needed to do was to weep in the presence of the emperor and have the scholars dismissed. Today the situation has not altered in its essentials. Only by fighting for a new principle as principle, will there be any chance of changing the state of affairs.

27

THE CALISTHENIC VALUE OF
KOWTOWING

THE Chinese word for "hygiene" must be taken in an entirely different sense from its usual acceptation in English. It, too, may be defined as "anything except sport," which, according to the Chinese, is a gratuitous waste of energy. I think my readers will take for granted the truism that the overexertion and overdevelopment of bodily organs involved in Western athletics is detrimental to one's health. It is all right for a man to be able to swing a golf stick and walk a few miles a day, but when a man breaks a hundred yards sprint record, it is a dead certainty—admitting exceptions, of course—that he won't be good for anything else. And there are things like "athlete's heart."

Chinese hygiene, on the other hand, throws its entire

emphasis on conservation of energy, and whatever forms of sport are prescribed or recommended, the great principle is always that of moderation. Whatever "exercise" there may be consists of harmonious movements calculated to normalize, but not to excite, one's bodily regimen. It starts out with mental regimen as the basis, in which the sole object is to bring about peace and calm of mind and spirit, and with this as the basis, it aims at stimulating a normal functioning of the internal processes of respiration and blood circulation. Hence there is the great science known as "sitting still," or *séance,* with such important details as keeping a straight bodily posture, rubbing the palms of the hands and the forehead, conscious and systematic swallowing of saliva, regulated respiration, and abdominal deep breathing according to a definite number of beats. Such internal regimentation promoting peace of the mind and body is the aim of Chinese hygiene.

In accordance with this theory of hygiene, the Chinese have developed types of movement characterized by slowness and rhythm, as all movements of a true gentleman should be. The art of kowtowing is but one of such movements. It is, in fact, the best exercise ever invented by the mind of man for the reducing of obesity.

In order to understand the art of kowtowing and its great calisthenic value, one should know first the principle of slow, rhythmic movement. The best example of such movement is perhaps to be found in the Chinese stage gestures, *t'aipu,* which are sometimes considered as important as vocal training to a Chinese actor. Now what is *t'aipu* except rhythmic, regulated, and stylized movement? In a perfect actor, these gestures and steps are timed perfectly with the rhythm of his words, so that we see a complete harmony of rhythmic language and rhythmic action. The rhythm in his speech is as clear and unmistakable as in his hand and leg movements. There is a graceful, punctuated rhythm in his laughter, his snorts, and even in his coughs and sneezes and spittings. I have sometimes tried to measure the beats involved in a Chinese gentleman's spitting, and found it almost invariably to be as follows: 1: 2: 3. The first two beats represent two perfectly timed inward movements of the nostrils in preparation for the spitting out, which occupies one half of the third beat. The drawing in is as sonorous and leisurely as the spitting out is quick and decisive. Now if one repeats this 1: 2: 3. movement successively, it could be aesthetically very satisfying. And try to transcribe the punctuated beats of a Chinese gentleman's laughter. The "attack" of the successive *"ha! ha! ha's!"* is extremely artistic and ingratiating, and there is usually a perfectly executed *crescendo,* losing itself in a generous broadening volume. And when a gentleman is displeased and leaves the room, it is generally preceded by that movement of jerking his sleeves, known in literature as *fohsiu.* The Chinese gentleman's sleeves are often rolled up once for work, resulting in the so-called "horse-hoof sleeves." When a gentleman is displeased, he generally gives his right-hand sleeve an energetic jerk downwards, which makes the folding come down, and with a rhythmic sweeping gesture of his arm, he waddles out of the room. No doubt his long gown helps to convert the jerky movements of his legs into a series of rounded and continuous hyperbolic movements. This is known as *tu fangpu.* In comparison with this gait, a foreigner's pantalooned movement is rough and vulgar.

Sufficient has been said to illustrate the aesthetic appreciation of slow rhythmic movements among the Chinese and enable foreign readers to understand what I mean by the calisthenic value of kowtowing. Kowtowing is but one form of greeting, only much more developed and dignified than other forms. There is, for instance, as much rhythm in the "curtsying" of eighteenth-century ladies and a modern German gentleman's clicking of heels and graceful bow. These things are always beautiful to look at. There is also beautiful rhythm in the *tach'ien* movement of a Manchu lady in Peiping. Sometimes she bends one of her knees and in that posture swings her body round on one heel and in this way gives her greeting to the entire company present in one graceful turn.

But let us come to kowtowing, the highest and most unique art of Chinese culture. Lord MacCartney, or whoever it was, refused to kowtow to Emperor Ch'ienlung because he was not aware that it was the most dignified and most hygienic posture a Chinese gentleman could possibly take. Different exercises have, of course, been invented by beauty experts for reducing ladies' obesity, but still I am quite sure none is quite so effective as kowtowing. Like rowing, it involves the muscles of the entire body. The placing of the body in a restful kneeling posture at once brings about peace of mind and banishes all worries. Then hold your chest erect with the two palms pressed against each other, as in the usual posture for saying "Paternoster" or singing "Ave Maria." Then, with a breast stroke, simulating the paddle movement, throw the arms apart and downwards, while you bring your body forward and downward until your head reaches the ground. Make three kowtows and raise yourself again to the erect posture as far as the upper part of the body is concerned. This act of raising and bending one's body gives a wonderfully beneficial exercise to the abdominal muscles and helps better than any massage to dissolve excessive fat around the belly. If done to careful timing, it encourages deep breathing and stimulates the blood circulation.

It is a pity that such a cultivated art should go to the dogs now. But there is a hopeful sign that along with other movements for the restoration of Chinese culture, like the encouragement of "chaste widows," this art will again be generally cultivated in a very short time, both among the high and low. I know this because I know that when the Manchu victorious army came to Pukow in 1644, a great scholar and Cabinet minister like Ch'ien Ch'ienyi knelt on the bank of the Yangtse on the Nanking side to welcome the conquerors, and kowtowed his way into a vice-ministership in the new alien regime. It is interesting to note, however, that in their hearts, the Manchu conquerors had nothing but utter contempt for Ch'ien, for when Emperor Ch'ien-lung was drawing up an *Index Expurgatoris,* Ch'ien's works ranked first among those to be burned, explicitly to discourage such shameful "duplicity." This was very unfair, because Ch'ien was such a beautiful writer.

28

CONFUCIUS SINGING IN THE RAIN

WITH all his shortcomings, inconsistencies, and often un-scrupulous conduct, Confucius remained a very charming character. The charm lies in his intense humanity and his sense of humor. Many of the sayings recorded in the *Analects* can only be properly understood in the nature of light humorous remarks between him and his intimate disciples. Once Tsekung said to him: "Here's a precious stone. It is concealed in a casket, waiting for a good price for sale."

And Confucius replied: *"For sale, indeed, for sale! I am the one waiting for sale!"* He was sometimes capable of wit, as when he said, *"If people don't say 'What shall I do? What shall I do?' indeed I don't know what I shall do with such people!"*

Another time, Confucius and his disciples had lost track of each other in the city of Cheng. Some one had seen Confucius standing at the East Gate, and told Tsekung, "There is a man at the East Gate, with a head like that of Emperor Yao, a neck like that of Kaoyao, and a shoulder like that of Tsets'an, but from the waist downwards he is shorter than Emperor Yu by three inches. He appears crestfallen like a homeless wandering dog." When they had found each other, and Tsekung had told the story to Confucius, the latter said, "The first part of the description is not quite right, but *'like a homeless wandering dog,'* indeed I am! indeed I am!" I believe here we have arrived at the true Confucius, erring, struggling, sometimes elated and sometimes despondent, but always retaining a personal charm and a good sense of humor, and able to laugh at a joke at his own expense. This is the true Confucius, and not the immaculate saint of irreproachable character which the Confucian scholars and the Western Sinologues would have us believe.

In fact, one can arrive at a true appreciation of the beauty of Confucius' character only through his humor. His was not the brilliant wit and satire of Chuangtse, but the mellow, kindly humor of resignation, which is more typically Chinese. For there is a beauty in Confucius' character which often escapes his critics and an intense charm and loveliness about the man which can be appreciated only at close range, such as in his intimate intercourse with his disciples. As far as I am concerned, the Confucius who has charmed me is not the great exponent of social order, nor the fiery young reformer who chopped off Shaocheng Mao's head, but the Confucius in his mellow middle age, when it was apparent that he was a political failure, and just before he gave up all political ambitions and decided to devote himself to learning and scholarly research.

There is a passage in *Shiki* recording a scene during this period of his life, which is comparable in its touching appeal to our emotions to the scene of the Gethsemane in the gospel, with the difference that it ends up in a note of humor, for Confucius was always able to laugh at himself. By this time, Confucius had wandered through many countries to seek the favor of some ruler who would put him in power and had met with humiliations and insults on every side. Twice he had been arrested, and once he starved with his disciples for seven days, for he had to leave one country after another like a mad prophet, despised, ridiculed, and unwanted. He left Ch'i in such a mad fury that he could not wait for the lunch which would be ready in half an hour, but carried the rice wet from the pan with him. At Wei, he had met the humiliation of parading the streets in a carriage following that of the Queen and having to admit to himself that "People loved beauty more than they loved virtue." When he was discoursing on benevolence and righteousness, the King of Wei turned his head up "to look at the flying wild geese" in the clouds. Then he was going to Chao across the Yellow River in Shensi for a political appointment, and again there was a hitch in the arrangement, and he had to stop on the brink of the Yellow River and exclaim: "Ah! How beautiful is the water! How magnificent it is! It must be Fate indeed that I am not able to cross this river!" And so he had wandered, away from Wei, back into Wei again, and left Wei a second time, and passed on to Ch'en, Ts'ai, Yeh, and P'u, followed by a handful of his sincere disciples, like a pack of wandering hobos. By this time his disciples were already showing disappointment and some slight resentment, but it is recorded that Confucius "retained his equanimity of temper and kept on teaching them and singing or playing on stringed instruments as usual." That was the time when, as *Shiki* says, Confucius was "mellow and resigned and didn't know what to do."

It was then that Confucius and his followers found themselves stranded in the country between Ch'en and Ts'ai, and their conversation here has always touched me profoundly. This was the turning point of Confucius, from which point on Confucius turned back in his journey and returned to his native country Lu to devote himself to the compilation of books.

Confucius knew that his disciples were displeased in their hearts, and he therefore asked Tselu to come in and asked him: "The ancient poem says, 'Neither tigers nor rhinoceroses, they wander in the desert.' Do you think my doctrine is wrong? Why is it I have come to this?" To this Tselu replied: "Perhaps our character is not benevolent (great) enough and we are unable to win people's confidence." Confucius said: "Can this be the case, Ah Yu? If the benevolent ones could always win people's confidence, why did Poyi and Shuch'i end up as they did? And if the wise ones could always win people's confidence, why did Prince Pikan have to be murdered?"

Thereupon Tselu left the room and Tsekung came in. Confucius said: "Ah Sze, the ancient poem says 'Neither tigers nor rhinoceroses, they wander in the desert.' Do you think that my doctrine is wrong? Why is it that I have come to this?" To this Tsekung replied: "Master, your doctrine is so great that the world cannot tolerate it. Why don't you come down a little from your height?" And Confucius said: "Ah Sze, a good farmer plants the grain but cannot guarantee the harvest; a good artisan can exercise his ingenuity but cannot guarantee success. A gentleman cultivates knowledge, arranges it in order and brings it into a system, and docs not care whether he is tolerated or not. Now you do not cultivate knowledge and desire only to be tolerated by people. You are not a man of great ambition!"

Thereupon Tsekung left the room and Yen Huei came in. Confucius said: "Ah Huei, the ancient poem says 'Neither tigers nor rhinoceroses, they wander in the desert.' Do you think that my doctrine is wrong? Why is it that I have come to this?" To this Yen Huei replied: "Master, your doctrine is so great, therefore the world cannot tolerate it. However, master, you just do your best to advocate it. Does it matter if you are not tolerated by the world? It is a sign of a gentleman that he is not tolerated by the people. If knowledge is not cultivated, it is our disgrace. But if we do cultivate our knowledge and the world will not listen to us, it is a disgrace of those in power. Does it matter if we are not tolerated by the world? It is a sign of a gentleman that he is not tolerated by the people." Confucius smiled happily and said: "You have said it! Thou son of Yen! If you were a rich man, I would be your butler!"

Confucius was singing in the rain and who can resist the charm of a person singing in the rain? For there he was, wandering in this desert with his disciples and coming to the end of their wits and not knowing where to go next, like a company of indescribable beggars or tramps, "neither tiger nor rhinoceros," and neither fish, flesh, nor good red herrings. And yet he still could afford a joke. There was no anger in his soul. I wonder that no Chinese painter has painted this scene in the desert which shows Confucius at his best.

29

KING GEORGE'S PRAYER

I ONCE read a code of conduct which King George V of England was said to have framed and hung up in his bedroom. Some interesting glimpses are thus obtained of the ideas that mold the English character. The royal prayer reads:

Teach me to be obedient to the rules of the game.
Teach me to distinguish between sentiment and sentimentality, admiring the one and despising the other.
Teach me neither to proffer nor to receive cheap praise.
If I am called upon to suffer, let me be like a good-bred beast that goes away to suffer in silence.
Teach me to win, if I may; if I may not, teach me to be a good loser.

Teach me neither to cry for the moon, nor to cry over spilt milk.

Here we have an intimate picture of the thoughts that are supposed to agitate a British king's breast—rather strange thoughts for a Chinese king, if we had a king. Whether that royal gentleman actually prayed every night in this fashion or not is a matter of no importance; so many modern gentlemen do not pray every night that we are warranted in supposing that the king had joined the ranks of the moderns. As Bernard Shaw insisted, the British king was chiefly loved because he was a modern gentleman and a nice sociable fellow, not because of his intellectual and moral pretensions. But the fact remains that the British king must have loved the beautiful sentiments expressed in these lines so much that he wanted to have them recorded and hung up in his bedroom, and that is as good as any nightly mumbling of prayers. In this plain text are expressed simply and deeply the ideals of fair play, sportsmanship, hatred of sentimentality, and strength of character that have distinguished the British people as a nation.

The fine maxims, however, do not apply to China, and a Chinese ruler's code of conduct would have to be drawn up along different lines. My Chinese ruler would probably get "stuck" on reaching the fifth word "obedient," and I should have to take fully a quarter of an hour to explain to him that there is no essential incongruity between a ruler and "obedience" to rules. "The rules of the game" would take me another quarter of an hour to explain. I would despair of making him understand the difference between sentiment and sentimentality; in fact I would not attempt it at all. And he might so hate me, when I rendered the plain sense of "not receiving cheap praise" that I would hesitate to proceed any further. He would ask me "Why not?" and I should be at a loss to explain. By this time, I should be so sick of explaining strange ideas to a successful and powerful man that I would rather murder the text and alter it to suit the hypothetical ruler's taste. I would go on in something like the following manner:

> If I am called upon to suffer, I would resign and let everybody know it is because of urinary disturbances.
> Teach me to win, if I may; if I may not, teach me to run away to the foreign concessions in good time, and read the classics.
> Teach me neither to cry for the moon, nor to cry over spilt milk, but to sing in times of failure——
> "Have Son: All Things Satisfactory,
> "No Office: One Body Light."

Sociologists tell us that different countries have different customs. Hence the roads to success are not the same in all countries. Certainly King George's bedroom prayer would not help any Chinese official in his advancement, and it simply would not do as a Chinese ruler's code of conduct. Were the new Machiavelli to write a collection of Sunny Thoughts to be hung up in our Chinese prince's bedroom and read by him every morning when he gets up, he would have to incorporate some of the wisdom contained in the following lines:

> Teach me to remember every general's birthday, and every general's mother's birthday, and teach me to send more important presents than just longevity noodles;

Teach me to value every human relationship as a political weapon, and consecrate marriage itself to the sacred claims of the State;

Teach me gentleness, urbanity, and good manners, that I may offend nobody and look as if butter would not melt in my mouth;

Teach me versatility and resourcefulness that I may have a good word for everybody and everybody will call me a good fellow;

Strengthen me in my gentility towards my foreign friends and give me dauntless courage against the people's protests;

Grant me valor in dealing with student demonstrations and inspire me with resolution in handling labor troubles;

Teach me oratory;

Teach me calligraphy;

Bless me with glibness of tongue and the power of rhetoric;

Inspire me with a sense of give-and-take, that I may neither spurn to proffer, nor disdain to receive, longevity presents;

Quicken me with a sense of the vanity of life, that I may make hay while the sun shines;

Endow me with a sense of humor, and guide me to see the farcicality of political life, that I be not overserious about anything;

Teach me to forgive and overlook the trespasses of my subordinates, as I wish my trespasses to be overlooked and forgiven;

Deliver me from public knowledge. Whatever happens, let me not be found out. . . .

30

THE COOLIE MYTH

CHINA is a land of myths. Some of them are very recent
creations. Like Bernard Shaw's plays, they can be divided
into two classes: Myths Pleasant and Unpleasant. There is,
for instance, a pleasant myth (current among the New York
intellectuals) that in China, we do not call our medical man
"doctor of medicine" but "doctor of health." "What a beautiful idea!" my New York hostess once exclaimed. "But it is
a beautiful misunderstanding only, madam," I was honest

enough to reply, for the term *I-sheng* means merely a "cure man" and not, as the Sinophile imagines, "one who cures you to life." Besides, what really matters is not the name, but what these doctors do to you. Since both Chinese and Western doctors' business is to put you in bed, it really does not matter by what name you call them. It is true that the Chinese have a greater genius for inventing beautiful names, and if such names represent beautiful thoughts, then we have plenty of them. The Europeans are very matter-of-fact, when they call a fire exit just a fire exit. The literary-minded Chinese consider such a name rather vulgar, and call it "world peace door" instead. That, however, does not alter the fact that I feel safer when I find the door marked "fire exit" than when it is marked "world peace door," because the latter is likely to call up in my mind a picture of a grand pandemonium, in case a fire does break out. Such myths, therefore, do not really mean anything.

There are other myths pleasant and unpleasant. A highly insulting and disparaging myth is that we Chinese eat *chop suey* and consider it a delicacy. The American lady who extols *chop suey* in the presence of Chinese friends is just making a fool of herself. We don't eat *chop suey,* because the things left over from regular feasts are generally given to servants only. There is really only one *chop suey* shop in Shanghai that made a reputation by collecting the left-overs from the restaurants and selling them to ricksha men at so many coppers per bowl. Now some connoisseurs have averred that such *chop suey* is really wonderful, but it is emphatically untrue that the Chinese residents in Shanghai are clients of that *chop suey* shop.

The Prince of Wales once credited us also with being the first inventors of the cinema. I do not know whether His

Royal Highness was referring to the rotating lantern, or the Pekingese shadow plays, most probably the latter. Now I confess we are an extremely clever people: we have invented the compass, paper, printing, and silk; we have invented gunpowder and also its proper use, which is to make fire-crackers for our grandfathers' birthday; we have invented the world-famous *mahjong* and the Chinese wire puzzles, including the nine-dragon-circles. We have done a lot of clever things, but if it is implied we have produced an inventive genius with a scientific discipline like Edison and can invent a thing like the cinema, the statement deserves to be classified among the pleasant myths.

We come now to the coolie myth. The coolie never existed in China. It is a European creation, and it exists only in the European mind. The Chinese language does not contain such a term. We have the term *chuo ku-li ti,* meaning "one who labors." But *ku-li* is never used as a noun, and it is not even an accepted Chinese phrase or idiom. And then one who labors is not a coolie; he is, or he was until the Europeans mentally degraded him, a respectable laborer, artisan, porter, waiter, carpenter, cabinet maker or what not. He may even be a house servant, but he is not a coolie in the Chinese language.

For there is that fine distinction between a "porter," "waiter," "butler," "servant," and a mere coolie. For a porter or a servant is a fellow human being, while a coolie is not. At least the distinction holds in the mind of the man who uses this word. A porter, for instance, is a man who shares the same belief in God with you and who talks a language you can understand. You can understand a porter, but you cannot understand a coolie, for you don't have to. You can talk with a servant, but you don't talk with a coolie—all you need is a pair of strong God-given calves and thick man-made boots. He will always understand that language. You would be ashamed of certain things before your servants, but you needn't be ashamed of doing the same things before a coolie. Then there is also that metaphysical question: Whereas St. Thomas Aquinas and his theologians have long established the fact that servants have souls, it is still open to question whether a coolie has a soul, or a sense of honor, or a sense of shame.

The coolie, therefore, does not exist as a class, except vis-à-vis the Europeans. Not all the Europeans have the same psychology, of course. There are among my foreign friends people who see a human touch in their coolies, who regard them as capable of shame, sorrow, humiliation, pain, pride, happiness, moodiness, and all those human emotions. But the general acceptance of the term has been more or less fixed, and the average speaker uses the term in the sense that early sailors, adventurers, and opium smugglers on the China coast used it in the nineteenth century. For that reason, Pearl Buck is all the greater when she, in a story "My Chinese Amah," presented the old amah of her childhood days as an ugly, superstitious but nevertheless kindly, big-hearted and well-bred human peasant woman that I would not be ashamed to call my own mother.

The "coolie" notion is so foreign to the Chinese mind that even a hundred years after the Europeans began to use it, we have not incorporated it into the Chinese language. We cannot express the notion today in Chinese. The notion exists therefore only among the English-speaking "higher-class" Chinese. To the higher-class Chinese, with the advantage of a Western education, a ricksha man may really be a coolie. But if he could read and write or even talk Chinese, the situation would be different. The moment he calls a wharf coolie not a coolie but a *hsiao-kung,* he is bound to call up a different image. For *hsiao-kung* may be poor and his lot may be hard but he is not a coolie. To a Chinese who understands him, he is a laborer, just the stuff of which the Chinese nation is made and the stuff which keeps the nation's industry and agriculture going in spite of all that the nation's gentry have been doing to prevent them from accomplishing anything.

Hard enough, yes, is the lot of many shop apprentices and child laborers. But I somewhat suspect there is a deeper humanity in the relationship between the apprentice and his master than that between the coolie and the European "boots." At least there is such a thing as manners between them. And every apprentice must still be "given face."

There is only one class of real coolies that I have been able to discover. But they are also a class that grew up after the Europeans came. They are a certain section of English-speaking Chinese, both of the higher and lower class, who are ashamed of their fellow brethren the ricksha pullers. They, too, have learned to use the boot-language and to dehumanize labor. They have thinner legs than the Europeans, but they, too, wear knickers. They may speak perfect academic English or merely pidgin, but they have begun to speak Chinese with an English accent. They are the real coolies.

31

BEGGARS

I ONCE shocked an educated Englishman by telling him
that I liked the beggars of London. It was a double shock
because he thought there were no beggars in London, and
because I pointed them out as a sign of England's greatness.
He wouldn't believe it, but I convinced him. He was one of
the generation grown up after the war, and one of that
human *genre* that believes his own people to be the most
cursedly stupid on earth. "What do you like about England?" he challenged.

I said, "I like your English girls treading with big strides on low-heeled walking shoes on Oxford Street and their fresh, healthy laughter in the London fog. I like also their ring of laughter in a cinema theater, so hearty and good to hear. There is something suggestive of independence and good cheer and grit in that laughter and in their walking gait. The same sense of independence and self-respect you can see in the beggars of London."

Of course, the Englishman would say there are no beggars in London. There are only old women selling matches around the street corners. The Englishman would not admit it, and the old women would not admit it themselves. For the Englishman, the beggars don't exist. Well and good, but for me, they do. But I was not thinking of the old women selling matches; I was thinking of the London counterpart of the crayon painters and scribblers on the sidewalks of Thibet Road and Avenue Edouard VII of Shanghai. This is locally called in Shanghai, *kao-ti-chuang,* or "making accusation briefs to (or on) the earth"—the last resort of unemployed scholars and painters, driven to exhibit their artistic and literary compositions at the street corners. But there is a difference, for while the Chinese sidewalk artists will tell you their sob stories, the London one tries to give you some little pleasure in return for that not impossible twopence you may throw into his cap.

For there are two ways of begging, one by an exhibition of misery and one by pleasing the passer-by in some humble way or other. I have seen at the Confucian Temple in Nanking a man of forty or thirty-five, weighing about a hundred fifty pounds, standing on the stomach of a girl of twelve, lying bent face up on the ground, silent as death. One should see the muscular tension on the face of that girl. I wish the clever exponents of the New Life Movement had seen that face, and they most probably all do, because they all frequent the Confucian Temple. The man would not descend from that girl's stomach forming the highest point of the curve of her bent body, and he called to people to have mercy on their misery and throw coppers. He forgot to point out that the stomach did not belong to him. At least the sword swallower is more honest in this respect. He also goes round begging for coppers, with the sword stuck down his mouth and his face a picture of pain and misery. But it is his own face and his own throat, and he exhibits some skill. The beggars exposing their sores to your face and occupying by some arrangement among themselves all the nine turnings of the "nine-bent bridge" in the old tea garden of the Shanghai Chinese city are most typical of the exhibition method. A whole chapter might be written of the frauds and methods of the Shanghai beggars.

I was therefore most impressed when I saw the London sidewalk painters trying to cheer me up with some maxim about hope and courage. There was a beggar on Guilford Street, near Russell Square. I have forgotten the maxims now. One was about the "early bird catching the worm." I thought it was magnificent of him to give me that thought, although I do not believe in the early bird nonsense, which makes working at midnight an impossibility. Another in Bloomsbury used to paint pictures of rose-covered homesteads and glowing sunsets and storm-tossed ships at sea with his color crayons. He even made a very clever caricature of the Prime Minister. A caricature of a premier by a beggar! I thought: He deserves a whole shilling. Down on King's Way, there was an unemployed journalist. I do not know whether he copied some of his pithy and witty comments from *Punch* and *Tit-Bits,* or evolved them from his own brain. His wide and full forehead was uncovered, for its cap lay on the roadside, behind a chalked "Thanks!" I have seen equally brilliant literary giants on the sidewalks of Avenue Edouard VII, and in fact met one near the Nanking Theater who wrote in what I considered good and straight idiomatic English. But he wasn't giving me anything in return, for he was talking about himself. There was one on Charing Cross above Cambridge Circus who was not so good, for he was howling against the injustice of the world, and he didn't get a penny from me. He was sour and bitter and there was no lightness in his touch. It was inhuman of me perhaps to expect an educated beggar not to show a little sourness in his sidewalk compositions, but I didn't like him because I didn't like him. I am for the Bloomsbury man, with his humor and his decency and his self-respect. To this day, his brilliantly colored crayon pictures of English rose-covered homesteads beneath the sickly jaundiced London sky remain as one of my most vivid memories of London.

32

A BUS TRIP

AS USUAL, I arrived just in time to stop the steam launch which was already moving off the jetty. I was going to Changchow, my home town and my Mecca. I had not been home for years, and few vagabonds returned to their fathers' homes with a keener delight than I did that December morning. From Amoy to Changchow was about thirty-five miles, and a motor road had been constructed and a bus line was running which was supposed to take us there in an hour and half. Such, I understand, is the great improvement of the country since my college days.

The steam launch was to take us from the Island of Amoy to the mainland connected with Changchow. Already

in the launch were some twenty fellow passengers, among
them two girl students and an ostentatiously dressed returned South-Sea merchant, wallowing in all the glories of
his gold wrist watch and gold-banded cigarette holder. He
was a man of about forty, somewhat oily-looking, but wearing socks, which reminded me it was severe winter in
Amoy. He talked in a stentorian voice, and in such a way
that everybody could or should listen to him. "Soerabaya
. . . Siam . . . Annam . . . Soerabaya . . ." The syllables rolled
from his lips like perfectly cut marbles. By his side was a
woman, quiet, modest, and not bad-looking, but wallowing
still more in the glories of her gold bracelets and a gold
chain with a locket that must have weighed about half a
catty. The girl students were eying the woman and giggling.
They had enormous woolen wraps about their shoulders,
which they used like Spanish shawls. This effect was en-
hanced by the fact that the girls wore very short skirts, so
that one could see nothing except the shawls and the legs.
The contrast between them and the South-Sea merchant's
wife was perfect. One was Old China and the others represented Modern China. And Modern China was giggling at
Old China. Modern China—or rather the two Modern
Chinas—had bobbed and marcelled hair.

Crossing this part of the Amoy Channel was usually a
treacherous affair, but the morning happened to be calm,
and instead of white-foamed billows, one saw only the mo-
bile countenance of the sea, smiling in peaceful golden rip-
ples. In a quarter of an hour, we arrived at Sungsu, the
point on the mainland where the motor road terminated.
There was a gigantic cliff overhanging the sea, on top of
which stood a big white oil tank and a residence house of
the Asiatic Petroleum Company. The cliff was about thirty

to forty feet high, and even on this calm morning, the ocean tide lashed noisily upon the rocks. In the cheerful sun, the cliff presented a wall of the finest pastel shades of clay-blue and purple, changing into bright terra cotta toward the bottom, while shading off into light gray toward the upper part, until it was covered with the verdant green of the hill at the surface, with ocean clouds sailing through the blue sky above. A most beautiful picture it was, and yet on a dark, stormy night, one could imagine this lonely cliff as a perfect setting for Grillparzer's *Hero and Leander,* in which Leander was to swim the channel, scale the rocks, and serenade shy, beautiful Hero. With a little stretch of imagination, one could transform the channel into the Hellespont and the Petroleum Tank into the tower where Hero saw her Leander, the storms of their passions syncopating with the crescendo of the howling winds and the tossing sea outside. Grillparzer himself would not have been surprised to find one morning the body of Leander washed ashore at the foot of the lonely rocks.

The steam launch having arrived, we bought our tickets, but there was no bus. There were three buses, but they were already packed full with soldiers. I understood that of the twelve buses of the company running, eight had been commandeered by "the Army." "Where are the buses?" I asked the station master. "They are hidden somewhere at a village near by. They will be here in a minute. There is no use sending for them now. Wait until we have despatched these *chiu-pa* first, else they will overrun any number of buses we may provide."

The soldiers went off, and very soon, indeed, the buses appeared. All the passengers scrambled into their seats. I was lucky to get into the one that first arrived and secured a front seat. The oily South-Sea merchant and his wife were on the same bus with me, but the two girl students had got into another one: the Modern Chinas had parted company with Old China. Very soon, I heard something like a row behind. Two soldiers had got in without tickets. They were told by the conductor to go to the ticket office and get their half-price tickets, but the soldiers refused, saying they would rather pay at their seats.

"What's the use of the ticket office, if everybody buys his ticket on the bus?" said the conductor. "There is plenty of time."

To my surprise, the soldiers each took a dollar piece grouchily from his pocket, and gave it to the conductor.

"Fukien is a rotten place!" one of them said in Honanese accent. "Communications are bad."

The oily merchant had got in without tickets, too. "You must study the people's psychology," he said, taking care to use the new terms "study" and "psychology." "It is natural that every one likes to get his seat first." By that instinct for moralization, I recognized the merchant as my true compatriot.

"Fukien is a rotten place!" re-echoed the soldier, but elicited no further comment from the merchant.

Our journey had an unlucky beginning. When the bus was about to start, the driver discovered that the spring of the clutch pedal had jumped off or was broken. Some minutes passed, with the driver, who was no mechanic, monkeying in vain with the pedal. With this pedal out of commission, it was impossible to shift the gear, and it would be necessary to run the bus the whole way in third gear. Since we had to climb up and down, the idea somewhat disheartened me, and I felt a little disconsolate. Bad omen at the beginning!

But the problem was how to get it started at all. A second bus was ordered to push our machine. Instead of getting a rope, which perhaps was not to be found, they used the second bus to give us a back kick, as it were, from behind. At every back kick, our machine jumped and the whole body creaked. Depreciation must be reckoned at 75 per cent per year, I thought to myself. But soon, on turning, the bus floundered into a sandy spot on the road. Some women and a little girl were scared out of their wits, and demanded to come down. The driver insisted that nothing was the matter, but, with one wheel stuck in the sand, it was found impossible to move the bus an inch. The oily merchant then decided that the little girl should have the "right" (another new term) to get down if she preferred to. As a matter of fact, all of us had to get off in order to lighten the load.

Finally, the bus was brought around, and we again clambered to our seats, the South-Sea merchant proposing—in fact ruling—that everybody should take his original seat. A new driver came to take the old driver's place, and while manipulating with the starter, suddenly found that he could start the car after all. Once started, there was no stopping him. But it was in third gear, and we remained in third gear during our journey. When I saw an up-grade in front of us where we had to go over a little elevation, I politely asked the driver how he was going to do it. "Shoot over at forty-five miles an hour," he said. And he did it. It turned out there were a succession of such elevations, as the country was a little hilly, and every time the driver took a delight in "shooting" over it at top speed, as the Honolulu surf riders shoot over the wave. "Very thrilling experience!" I assured the driver, who was a sort of daredevil scamp, with one red eye and a woolen knitted cap shaped like the half of an orange.

This arrangement went pretty well for some time until we reached a station, when some passenger got down. The machine then not only refused to start, but the engine would not even run.

"Mutual help!" shouted the South-Sea merchant, and suggested that the next bus should be made to tow us. But where was the rope? Luckily, we found some wire of fair size at the station; this was made four strong and attached to the two buses, which were separated by a distance of some thirty feet. Before we started, however, a fellow appeared with calendars of some Japanese flour company, and distributed them gratis, shouting "Old Calendar! Old Calendar!" There was a general scramble at this unexpected signal. Even the station master ran out of his house to secure a copy. The Old Calendar was, by the way, a prohibited but extremely desirable article in the country.

So we started again. The first bus went jauntily ahead, towing us. It was found, however, that it was difficult to make the four wires of exactly equal length, so that, in reality, the whole weight of the bus rested usually on one wire alone, instead of on four. At a sharp bend, followed by a descent, there was a sudden jerk and the wire snapped. We had then three wires left, but as these weren't tied any better than the last time, very soon another snapped again. The remaining wires were also by this time considerably shortened. This was repeated until the two buses were separated only by about twenty feet. The two might at any time collide. My heart was in my mouth.

"Better be careful," I told our driver.

"Don't be afraid," replied the red-eyed daredevil driver. "I want my life, too."

"But you aren't married, and I am," I remonstrated.

This gave an opening for the moralizations of the merchant and the passengers, who eventually won, and we abandoned the idea of reaching Changchow for lunch. At the next snap, the other bus was allowed to go ahead, with the understanding that it would come back and take our passenger load. We stood still. While waiting, the passengers engaged in a discussion on the merits of the old Changchow-Amoy Railway. The railway, by the way, once received an honorable mention in the *Encyclopaedia Britannica*. But it had been eaten up by some Foochow rats and the rats' cousins and rats' brothers-in-law. I had noticed, on passing Sungsu, still some bones on the railway cars, left over by the Foochow rats. That is sufficient evidence there is no use for other rats to try to chew them now. I thought I had seen the skeleton of half a car still standing on its feet. I do not know whether the Fourteenth American Edition of the *Encyclopaedia* still keeps that mention or not, but if it does, it should be taken out. The rats have chewed up and digested its meat long ago.

There was a story about a passenger's asking the engineer to wait for him while he finished his noodle in the restaurant. The engineer told him the train could not wait, but it would be all right if he finished his noodle first and then caught up.

At two o'clock, the other bus appeared and we changed over, and left for Changchow. To this day, I have not forgotten the face of the oily merchant or the red-eyed driver.

月餅

33

LET'S LIQUIDATE THE MOON

THE moon has become the object of much literary contentions in contemporary Chinese literature. She is not exactly the bone of literary contentions, but she waxes and wanes in favor of the different schools; both the "leftist" writers and the people they attack have at one time or another announced their intention to discuss only the "moon"; editors have begged their contributors to "talk less of politics and more of the moon and the wind"; and now, for no reason whatsoever, except that I am advocating development of the familiar, conversational style of writing in Chinese—carrying on the tradition of a few Chinese "Elias"—the communists have decided that the moon is going to ruin China, and that consequently we must liquidate the moon, if China is to be saved from the demoralizing influence of Lin Yutang. To Western readers not familiar with the Chinese communists' line of reasoning, I must inform them that they are all of the opinion that "humor will ruin China." Little do they suspect—and nothing makes them smart so much as when I point it out—that, although they seem to be so advanced in their thinking, in spirit they are nothing but remnants of the humorless fustian Sung Confucianists.

So I am forced to rally to the defense of the moon and prevent the moon from becoming liquidated. For I am truly afraid that when the Chinese as a nation have lost their capacity for enjoying the moon or a common plebeian summer breeze, the nation, as a nation, will become infinitely smaller and coarser and more materialistic. We have today already come to the point when for a man to look at the midautumn moon and eat the moon cake is to be "feudalistic" and "counter-revolutionary" because the moon cake is Chinese and therefore old-fashioned, while to eat Swiss nut-milk chocolates with some girl student is to be progressive, and "revolutionary," because nut-milk chocolates come from the West. Let them eat their Swiss chocolates, these wise young boys, in sublime disregard of the moon. But the moon will shine upon them, and she will continue to shine upon them, quietly, silently, without offering a self-defense, and one day she will win them over. Unless they are lost souls indeed!

The moon therefore cannot be liquidated as easily as the young writers think. Nor can T'ao Yuanming and Su Tungp'o and Tu Fu and Li Po, whom the communists equally desire to eliminate. "Poison" is the word they use. But T'ao Yuanming and Su Tungp'o will not be liquidated so long as the Chinese nation remains true to itself and true to its own genius. For all I know the communist youths do not even read Su Tungp'o or T'ao Yuanming. They call these writers "feudalistic" and "leisure class" and scholars "who do not face reality"—T'ao Yuanming, who sings of "picking chrysanthemum flowers along the eastern hedge-row" and "cocks perching on mulberry trees" and Su Tungp'o, who sings of "the fine breeze on the river and the clear moon on the mountains": feudalistic indeed! Are the mountain moon and the river breeze owned only by the capitalist leisure class? Do only capitalist cocks know how to perch on mulberry trees in the homes of millionaires? And are not cocks and mulberries part of the world of "reality"? The fact is, T'ao Yuanming and Su Tungp'o have advanced far beyond the stage of talking about the masses and plebeians—they have become great plebeians themselves and feel and think in harmony with the peasants.

The moon, therefore, cannot be liquidated. Let us rather liquidate the general question of the moon once and forever. The moon is connected with Chinese poetry and the familiar Chinese essay and with a peculiar type of Chinese romanticists. This type of Chinese romanticists is unknown to the West.

Chinese romanticists are different from the romanticists in the West. Western romanticists suggest violent, 'stormy passions, while Chinese romanticists suggest sweet and calm repose, concealing nevertheless a very rich sentimentality in their breasts. The Chinese name for this is *fengya,* an adjective composed of the two words "wind" and "elegant." It implies artistic cultivation, love of poetry, a carefree, easy-going personality with little concern for money, a great fondness for friendship, and generally a contempt for officialdom. Shen Fu, the author of *Six Chapters of a Floating Life,* and his friends at the Hsiaoshuanglou were true types of *fengya* people. Typical is Shen Fu's description of these friends:

> Among the friends at Hsiaoshuanglou, four things were tabooed: firstly, talking about people's official promotions; secondly, gossiping about lawsuits and current affairs; thirdly, discussing the conventional eight-legged essays for imperial examinations; and fourthly, gambling. Whoever broke any of these rules was penalized to provide five catties of wine. On the other hand, there were four things which we all approved: generosity, romantic charm, free and easy ways, and quietness.

These friends all dabbled in poetry and painting, drank, but not to excess, and loved friendship and conversation. Nothing delighted them more than a small unpretentious dinner under the moonlight. Poor and generous to a fault and happy they were, but capitalist running dogs they were not. Chinese romanticists were always men with a strong contempt for money and power, people who saw enough about the farce of social and political life not to tolerate even talking with a snobbish monk.

"How is everything at the city? And is the Governor still at his yamen?" inquired a monk whose temple Shen Fu's friends were casually visiting.

"The baldhead snob!" snorted one of Shen Fu's friends, and with a brushing of his long sleeves, he swept out of the room.

But underneath this carefree romanticism, the Chinese romanticists in history were men noted for their bravery in times of crisis and integrity during their brief official life.

Su Tungp'o, Po Chuyi, Yuan Mei, Cheng Panch'iao (that queer bird and eccentric genius), and Yuan Chunglang— one and all, they left a much cleaner record than the Confucian Pecksniffs who always spoke in large mouthfuls of benevolence and righteousness. They were true "parents" of the people when they were magistrates, and when these people departed from their posts, the peasants stood or knelt for miles round around their sedan chairs, shedding tears of gratitude and farewell. "Ah, you write so many poems about sing-song girls and so few poems about the people," sneered one of the doctrinaire Confucianists at Po Chuyi. On the surface, the Confucianists had the interests of the people at heart, but Po Chuyi was clean as an official, while the Confucianists were not. Chin Shengt'an, that distinguished critic of the seventeenth century, was called blasphemous by his orthodox critics, but it was he who could not endure the oppression of the poor and, on the occasion of an illegal taxation, staged a farmers' revolt by weeping with his friends at the Temple of Confucius, and consequently went heroically to his death for it. It was he who turned out on the side of the poor, and not the high official who sentenced him to his death on the ground of "disrespect to the emperor" and "disturbing the repose of the deceased emperor's soul" by crying at the Temple of Confucius during the hundred days of the emperor's mourning. Overtaxation of the peasants left that high official's soul in peace, and according to his interpretation, should also leave the deceased emperor's soul in peace. I prefer at any time the moon to the sanctimonious odor of these Confucian patriots!

狗肉將軍

威司

34

IN MEMORIAM OF THE DOG-MEAT
GENERAL

GENERAL CHANG TSUNGCH'ANG, the "dog-meat
general," had died, according to the morning's news. I was
sorry for him and I was sorry for his mother and I was sorry
for the sixteen concubines he left behind him and the four
times sixteen that had left him before he died. As I intended
to specialize in writing *in memoriams* for the bewildering

generals of this bewildering generation, I began with the Dog-Meat General first:

So our Dog-Meat General has died! What an event! It is full of mystic significance for me and for China and us poor folks who do not wear boots and carry bayonets! Such a thing could not happen every day, and if it could, there would be an end to all China's sorrows. In such an eventuality, you could abolish all the five *Yuan*, tear up the will of Dr. Sun Yat-sen, dismiss the hundred odd members of the Central Executive Committee of the Kuomintang, close up all the schools and universities of China, and you wouldn't have to bother your head about communism, fascism and democracy and universal suffrage and emancipation of women, and we poor folks would still be able to live in peace and prosperity.

So one more of the colorful, legendary figures of medieval China has passed into eternity. And yet Dog-Meat General's death has a special significance for me, because he was the most colorful, the most legendary, the most medieval, and, I must say, the most honest and unashamed of all the colorful, legendary, medieval, and unashamed rulers of modern China.

He was a born ruler such as modern China wants. He was six feet tall, a towering giant, with a pair of squint eyes and a pair of abnormally massive hands. He was direct, forceful, terribly efficient at times, obstinate, and gifted with moderate intelligence. He was patriotic according to his lights and he was anti-communist, which made up for his being anti-Kuomintang. All his critics must allow that he wasn't anti-Kuomintang from convictions, but by accident. He didn't want to fight the Kuomintang; it was the Kuomintang that wanted to fight him and grab his territory, and, being an honest man, he fought rather than turn tail. Given a chance and if the Kuomintang had returned him his Shantung, he would have joined the Kuomintang, because he said the Sanmin doctrine can't do any harm. He could not be anti-Kuomintang, because he couldn't be anti-something-that-he-didn't-understand. He could drink and he was awfully fond of "dog-meat" and he could swear all he wanted to and as much as he wanted to, irrespective of his official superiors and inferiors. He made no pretense to being a gentleman and didn't affect to send nice-sounding circular telegrams, like the rest of them. He was ruthlessly honest, and this honesty made him much loved by all his close associates. If he loved women, he said so, and he would see foreign consuls with a Russian girl sitting on his knee. If he held orgies, he didn't try to conceal them from his friends and foes. If he coveted his subordinate's wife, he told him openly and wrote no psalm of repentance about it like King David. And he always played square. If he took his subordinate's wife, he made her husband the chief of police of Tsinan. And he took good care of other people's morals. He forbade girl students to enter parks in Tsinan and protected them from the men-gorillas who stood at every corner and nook to devour them. And he was pious and he kept a harem. He believed in polyandry as well as polygamy, and he openly allowed his concubines to make love with other men, provided he didn't want them at the time. He respected Confucius. And he was patriotic. He was reported to be overjoyed to find a bedbug in a Japanese bed in Beppo, and he never tired of telling people of the consequent superiority of Chinese civilization. He was very fond of his executioner, and he was thoroughly devoted to his mother.

Many legends were told about Dog-Meat's ruthless honesty. He loved a Russian prostitute, and his Russian prostitute loved a poodle, and he made a whole regiment pass in review before the poodle to show that he loved the prostitute that loved the poodle. Once he appointed a man magistrate in a certain district in Shantung, and another day he appointed another man to the same magistracy. Both men therefore arrived at the same office and started a quarrel. Each claimed that he had been personally appointed by General Dog-Meat. It was agreed, therefore, that they should go and see the General to clear up the difficulty. When they arrived, it was evening and General Chang was in bed in the midst of his orgies. "Come in," he said, with his usual candor. The two magistrates then explained that they had both been appointed by him to the same district. "You fools!" he said, "can't you settle such a little thing between yourselves but must come to bother me about it?"

Like the heroes of *Shui-hu,* and like all Chinese robbers, he was an honest man. He never forgot a kindness, and he was obstinately loyal to those who had helped him. His trouser pockets were always stuffed with money, and when people came to him for help, he would pull out a bank roll and give a handful to those that asked. He distributed hundred-dollar notes as Rockefeller distributed dimes.

Because of his honesty and his generosity, he was beyond the hatred of his fellow men. The morning I entered my office and informed my colleagues of the great news, every one smiled, which showed that everyone was friendly toward him. No one hated him and no one could hate him. China was then still being ruled by men like him, who hadn't his honesty, generosity, and loyalty. He was a born ruler, such as modern China wants, and he was the best of them all.

35

THE LOST MANDARIN

ONE of the greatest calamities of the Chinese Republic is the disappearance of the former mandarin. I have been searching for rare specimens of this gentleman amidst the present ruins of the Manchu Empire. For he, I believe, is one of the finest fruits of Chinese culture.

The Manchu Dynasty may have been corrupt, yes, unbelievably corrupt, but those Manchu government crooks were superb polished gentlemen. Such mandarin were the product of centuries of culture, refinement, and tradition. A perfect mandarin was perhaps as rare as a perfect beauty. That lies in the nature of things. But we had at least scores of good mandarins at any period, whereas today we have only loyal party comrades. A mandarin was a real polished gentleman. We had scores of them, and they were worth having. In spite of the deep degradation of his soul, his presence was a delight to others, and his manners were a tribute not only to himself but also to those who offered him the bribe. His voice was deep and resonant, his bearing poised and calm, his language was an art, and his personality was a combination of scholarship, suavity, rascality, and high breeding.

It is perhaps as futile to define a mandarin as it is to define a gentleman. He is there, an incontrovertible fact of the universe, constantly provoking and defying definition. But you know a mandarin when you hear him talk, as you can tell a gentleman from the way his hair is parted. In the case of a gentleman, there is something in the ring of his voice and the carriage of his shoulders which gladdens and excites the feminine heart. And how many foreigners were charmed by the beard of Li Hungchang or by the eyes of Yuan Shih-kai! How many regret that such beings exist no more!

In order to know a true mandarin, you had only to hear him talk. He talked, of course, mandarin. Time was when talking mandarin was an art—an art that could be enjoyed for its own sake and which took half a lifetime to cultivate to perfection. Not that it was all a matter of accent, like the Oxford drawl, which any fairly intelligent child could pick up in three months. True, accent played an important part. Somewhere back in my memory I hear the deep, resonant voice of his language, the beautiful undulated rhythm of his Pekingese accent, punctuated by well-timed and equally rhythmic laughter. How one would die to hear such perfect mandarin discourse again! For if those mandarins robbed the people, they robbed nicely and politely and made the whole process seem pleasant and refined to the victim as well as to themselves. Now things are different. Our modern officials can only lie and lie in the most uncouth, impudent, incompetent, and immoral fashion. If we must be robbed, at least make it possible for us to enjoy it. But we can't even do that. That is why the disappearance of the mandarin is so great a calamity.

But if talking mandarin were all a matter of accent, it would not be worthy of the name of art. Like all art, it required an intellectual and moral background in the artist. In a perfect mandarin discourse, everything was harmonious; the personality of the speaker, the furniture of the room, the atmosphere of decorum, the tone of his voice, the perfect accent and refined phraseology, the round silken fan, the mandarin mustache and the *makua*—all united to give that harmonious artistic effect. No one can talk mandarin in Western dress, for the accompanying gestures are against it. It would be disastrous, for instance, to hold a round silken fan while wearing a golf mackintosh, or to blow the nose with a handkerchief while talking the imperial language. Instead of blowing the nose, one should cough and spit, cough and spit in the most approved fashion. Then there is the mandarin beard, which sometimes takes half a lifetime to grow to any imposing degree. I can think only of Yu Yujen as satisfactory in this qualification. Thirdly, there is the calm of discourse, the tone of voice and the mental poise, which presupposes a dignified and poised personality. And a dignified and poised personality requires a well-fed and complacent soul, which again requires learn-

ing, calm, experience, and courage. A mandarin may be disgraced, but he is never undignified. He groaned elegantly
and sneezed methodically. If he fell on the floor, the first
thing he did on getting up was to readjust his tortoise-shell
spectacles—leisurely, correctly. Our modern ministers look
as if they could even kick a football. Kicking a football is
a highly undignified bodily attitude. . . . Some even smoke
cigars. Now how can one smoke a cigar and talk mandarin?
The water pipe is the thing. As a matter of fact, I know
no officials who even attempt to talk proper mandarin. They
talk a Cantonese-Soochow-Wusih hybrid variety. Really it
is just as well. . . .

Last of all, talking mandarin requires a special phraseology. That phraseology is partly technical and partly literary. So far as it is technical, some of our government clerks
can still teach it to their ministers, because they know the
stuff. And if our ministers are intelligent they can easily
learn it. Those things are really very delightful to learn.
For instance, when you speak of your own son, call him a
"puppy," and when you refer to the other's son, call him a
"tiger." Again, your own wife is only "cheap thistle" while
your friend's wife is "madame." To ask a man to come to
your house tell him just to "order the carriage and gloriously
descend." Such polite distinctions make one really feel educated. They improve the mind.

But so far as the phraseology is literary, I don't advise our
ministers even to attempt it. It means hard study and real
grinding for a couple of decades. That is why a perfect
mandarin discourse was so rare and so delightful when you
found it. No matter what you say against the mandarin, he
had, in most instances, a fair knowledge of Chinese history,
literature, and *shuo-wen,* and he could repeat scores of liter-

ary essays and poems by heart. A really perfect mandarin conversation was a literary discourse. The speaker was at home in ethics and in political problems. For the Chinese mandarin was not just a courtier of the French type. He was by profession a scholar. He talked like a scholar. He had a public political philosophy and a private ethical philosophy. He was courtier and scholar combined. You could discourse with a first-class mandarin on Hsuntse, Motse, Yuan dramas, Sung ethics, and Ming porcelain. And our modern officials can only talk of wheat loans, twenty miles per gallon and 2½ per cent.

Yes, gone are the days of the mandarin, and decayed is the art of lying. Instead of a Li Hungchang we have a graduate of Columbia. We have generals who call themselves "Luck-lucky" (Fu-hsiang), "Gold and Jade" (Chin-yu), "Lucky Unicorn" (Fu-lin), and their concubines have sing-song names of sing-song origin, like "Miss Pearl and Miss Spring." It is humiliating that we should be robbed by these men.

Only the other day I met a person who had the make-up of a real mandarin. He was well fed. He had a copy of Ssuma Kuang's *Mirror of History* in his hands. He loved history and poetry and calligraphy. And he talked perfect mandarin with perfect accent, with that sureness for words which marked him off as a well-read man. I heard him talk —it was delightful—on the poverty of the people, the immorality of officials, the fearful effects of the movies, the importance of Confucian ethics, and the great need of a well-organized civil service system. His discourse was so smooth that I said to myself, "Here is the last of the mandarins, with the mandarin's scholarship, suavity, rascality, and high-breeding." He could be a big official and he could be dishonest. China might still be saved.

36

I LIKE TO TALK WITH WOMEN

I LIKE to talk with women. They are delightful. They always remind me of the immortal lines of Byron:

> What a strange thing is man! and what a stranger
> Is woman!

Now it must not be inferred that I am a misogynist, like Nietzsche and Schopenhauer; nor do I entertain that high notion of the ladies which is embodied in Shakespeare's gentlemanly saying, "Frailty, thy name is woman."

I like women as they are, without any romanticizing and without any bitter disillusionment. With all their contradictions, light-mindedness, and superficialities, I have an immense faith in their common sense and their instinct for life —their so-called sixth sense. Beneath their superficiality, they live a deeper life and are closer to this business of living than men, and I respect them for it. They live life, while men talk about it. They understand men, while men never understand women. While men spend their lives smoking or hunting or inventing or composing music, they bear children and provide for them, and that is a great thing. I do not believe there is a single father in the world who could provide for his children if left alone. If there were no mothers in this world, all children would catch measles and die of it in their first three years or turn pickpockets in their tenth year. Children would go late to school, and I doubt very much grown-ups would ever arrive in their office punctually. Handkerchiefs would remain unwashed, umbrellas would be lost, and bus lines would run irregularly. There would be no birthday parties, much less funeral processions, and certainly no barber shops. Yes, this great business of living and going on living until the tender flame of life flickers out is carried on by women and not by men. Through them and through them alone, do we preserve our racial continuity, our national homogeneity and our social solidarity. In a world without women, there would be no customs, no conventions, no churches, and no such thing as respectability. No man is inherently respectable, but all women are by nature. Instead of respectable and fairly standardized apartment flats and villas, men would live in triangular houses with the most inventive designs, in which one would eat in the bedroom and sleep in the parlor, and the best attachés would not be able to conceive of the importance of distinguishing between a white and a black tie.

Having made clear the superiority of women's instinct to men's logic, I may now explain why women are so delightful to men in their conversation. In fact, their conversation is part of their business of living. Instead of a colorless discussion of abstract terms, we have what is called gossip, in which persons are very real and everything either creeps or crawls or marries. A woman never introduces a professor of ichthyology in society as a professor of ichthyology, but as the brother-in-law of Colonel Harrison, who died in India while she was lying in hospital in New York after an operation for appendicitis. From this standpoint, she could launch forth into what the Japanese statesmen call "realities," with immense possibilities for development: Either Colonel Harrison used to take strolls with her in Kensington Gardens or the appendicitis reminded her of her "dear, old Doctor Brown, with his nice, long beard." No matter how high-flown the discussion may be, a woman always sticks to facts. She knows what are living facts, and what are useless, idle suppositions. That is why any real woman would, like the girl in *Gentlemen Prefer Blondes* when she visits Place Vendôme in Paris, prefer to turn her back on the monument and look up to the famous historical names like Coty and Cartier. Now what is the Vendôme, and what is Coty? With her sureness of instinct, she knows that Coty means something in life, while the Vendôme does not. In the same way, appendicitis is real, while ichthyology is not. Life is made up of births, deaths, appendicitis, measles, Coty's perfumes, and birthday parties, and not of ichthyology or ontology. Of course, there are Madame Curies and Emma Goldmans and Beatrice Webbs. But I am speaking of Woman, with a capital letter. I will give an instance:

"——is a great poet," I said once to a lady in a railway compartment. "He has a great ear for music, and his language seems to come so naturally."

"Do you mean W——? His wife smokes opium."

"Well, he did himself, occasionally. But I was talking about his language."

"She led him into it. I think she spoiled his life for him."

"Would you like your cook's pastry the less because he eloped with another man's wife?"

"Oh, that's different."

"It is exactly the same, isn't it?"

"I *feel* it is different."

When a woman appeals to her feeling, the wise man knows it is final, and should hand her the laurels.

37

SHOULD WOMEN RULE THE WORLD?

SOME American woman has launched the "beautiful thought" that men have made a mess of ruling the world, and that hereafter we should turn over the government of the world to women.

Now, speaking as a male human being, I am all for it. I am tired of ruling the world, and would gladly turn it over to anyone who is fool enough to relish the job. I want a vacation. I am an utter failure. I don't want to rule the world any more. I am sure all sane-minded men share the sentiment with me. I don't mind turning over the job to the natives of Tasmania, if they want it. My suspicion is that they don't.

I feel, and I am sure all my fellow men agree with me, that uneasy lies the head that wears a crown. It is alleged that we men are masters of our destiny and of the world's destiny, that we are captains of our souls and of the world's soul, that the world's best jobs, like being statesmen, politicians, mayors, judges, theater managers, owners of chocolate shops, and so on, have all been occupied by men. As a matter of fact, none of us likes it. The situation is simpler than that. In the words of a professor of psychology at Columbia University, the real division of job between men and women is that men have been earning all the money and women have been spending all the money. I am all for a change of the situation. I would like to see women slave at dockyards and business offices and conferences, while we men sit outside at our bridge parties in our delightfully cool green afternoon dress, waiting for our dears to come out from office and take us to cinemas. That, I say, is a beautiful thought.

But apart from such selfish reasons, we really ought to be ashamed of ourselves. The world couldn't be possibly worse ruled or misruled than it has been ruled by us men. So when women say, "Us girls should have a chance, too," why not be honest, admit our failure, and turn it over to the girls?

"Them girls" have been rearing all the babies, and we men go ahead and start wars and kill the best of them. It is really horrid. But there is no help for it. We men are born like that. We must fight, while women only scratch each other, which cannot cause more serious damage than surface bleeding. If blood poison does not set in, there's really no harm done. Women are satisfied with rolling pins. But we must fight with machine guns. It has been said that so long as men like to hear brass bands we must fight. We can't resist the brass bands. Suppose we sit quiet a little and stay at home and get used to afternoon parties, do you think we would fight any more? In a world where women rule, we could say to them, "Now you girls, you are ruling the world, so if you want war, you go and fight yourselves." There will be no machine guns, then, and the world will be at peace at long last.

We really ought to be ashamed of ourselves. Economic conferences failed. Disarmament conferences failed. Man has failed. Everybody knew that we had to get together and stop warfare and arrange so that we could trade peacefully with each other. But what did we do? Instead of sending our best brains to conferences, men like Albert Einstein and Bertrand Russell and Romain Rolland, we handed the whole matter to "experts." We sent army experts and navy experts, men who love not peace but wholesale murder, to the disarmament conference, and then we wondered why the conference failed! The next thing was that we wanted to relieve the depression, promote world trade, and abolish the war debts, and what did we do? We sent a lot of professors of economics and statisticians and specialists in love with their tariff barriers, and then we wondered why the economic conference failed! It is almost as bad as trying to simplify the English language by calling a conference, not of writers, but of grammarians, men who are in love with their conjugation tables, and expecting them to make a success of it.

Now I don't care what happens. While men talked in

white kid gloves, the war clouds loomed. When the girls say they want to try, I say "Go to it, and may God bless you! You can't possibly make a worse job of it than I have."

So for my part, I am going to resign and hand over the government of the world to the Broadway babies and older girls, and if I can save enough money, I am going to hide myself in the South Sea Islands or the African jungles. And when civilization goes up in a gigantic, spectacular conflagration, I can say to myself on top of an African tree, "Oh God, at least I have been honest with myself."

姑娘

38

IN DEFENSE OF CHINESE GIRLS

An Open Letter to a French Writer

DEAR M. DEKOBRA:

Things have happened since I last saw you at Yufengtai, the Shaohsing wine shop on Foo-chow Road, where we had, besides crabs and wine, the company of some of Shanghai's élite madonnas, and where, thinking of your "Madonna of the Night Express," I suggested to you to write a sketch on

"Crabs and Madonnas," but you disdained the crabs and preferred to listen to the madonnas. The wine was excellent, and the crabs were delicious (although you were entirely unaware of it), and the Chinese madonnas were charming and beautiful. Some of the flavor of the night still remains with me. As I was sitting there, I could not help thinking that you had the privilege of observing modern Chinese women at their best and that this fact might change your entire outlook on Chinese womanhood. I did not know that you were going to be carried away by your enthusiasm and land yourself in trouble by your inordinate praise of Chinese women. And now some of our Peiping college girls are howling at you for saying nothing more offensive than that they are beautiful. You are probably at a loss to understand yourself how this trouble came about, and I am offering to help you out by analyzing the psychology of the Chinese college girls for you.

Now, I have not met a single European visitor of the artist type who did not give his opinion that the Chinese girls are supremely beautiful in their poise and refinement and that their dress, too, has a charm and witchery of line not found in European ladies' dress. But, so far as I know, you are the first man to come out and openly declare that the Chinese girls are beautiful. It is reported that you have the bad taste to like both Chinese food and Chinese girls, and, worse than that, there is the possibility of your one day abandoning your confirmed bachelorhood and marrying one of them. Such an unusual statement is unheard of in the Chinese press. Now, we have never heard a Shanghai European praising Chinese food or Chinese dress or Chinese buildings or Chinese women, or if I personally have, the Chinese public as a whole are unaware of it. Some Britishers have confessed privately and in shame that they really like Chinese food, but no decent Englishman could make a statement in the Shanghai Club that he likes Chinese food or Chinese women or the Chinese people in general without being regarded as "queer" and at once losing caste. . . . The thing has gone so far that the Chinese people themselves are afraid of eating their food in their own way in the presence of foreigners or wearing their own long gowns or talking their own language, or owning a Chinese-style garden. And now you have the audacity to come and tell us that Chinese girls are beautiful. Of course, nobody will believe you, least of all the Chinese girls themselves. The sophomore girls refuse to believe in you. Miss Pan, who led the boycott against you in Peiping, says of course you are sarcastic. Of course you are joking, and—this is what makes it unbearable—you are mocking at them. A girl writer in the *Tawanpao* asks, Why do you mock at Chinese, and not at Parisian women? Miss Pan demands to know why you don't talk of literature instead only of girls (a typically sophomoric question). A male contributor to the *China Times* gives a heart-searching question: Why don't you insult the ladies of other countries, but choose to insult Chinese girls? Isn't this food for thought for the Chinese girls themselves? And the echo of a woman writer in the *Tawanpao* is pathetic in its sincerity: Although we do not choose to be insulted by anybody, still we ourselves are to blame. Oh, sisters, we must wake up. . . . All this because you say (according to *Shun Pao*) that the ideal woman for you is a gay, Oriental beauty!

No, we have been so bullied and bamboozled and disheartened that we can't believe anybody who says a good thing of China. We have gone so far now that when we see a foreign visitor standing transplanted and spellbound before the Temple of Heaven, we have a feeling the Temple of Heaven ought to bow its head in shame. We are inwardly sorry it isn't built of reinforced concrete, and that it has only three stories. And if the foreigner should call it beautiful, the Temple of Heaven would, if it were a human being, like Miss Pan, say to him in protest "You cannot be serious," if not accuse him of downright intentional insult. It's like a slave girl who, ill-treated all her life, suddenly finds somebody patting her on the back, and shouts in amazed anger, "How dare you!" But you have dared, Monsieur Dekobra. There is now no way to make them believe you except by keeping on saying and saying again that "Chinese girls are beautiful." And when the next European novelist comes along and concurs in your opinion, his cross may be made a little lighter for him.

Of course, you know what I have been driving at. The phrase "inferiority complex," trite as it is, involuntarily crops up. As a novelist, you know of course that an inferiority complex can very well exist without actual inferiority. All you need is to tell a man that he is no good ten times a day, and very soon he begins to believe it himself. That is how Sunday schools turn out so many "children of Beelzebub"— just by telling boys and girls they are that when they like red ribbons or sweets—and they will go home like criminals and tell their parents, to their great embarrassment, that they are children of Beelzebub. Your white brothers in the Far East, Monsieur Dekobra, are the Sunday School gospellers who by their clean-shaven superiority and by their hatred of dirt and the yellow skin and the flat face make us think we are children of the devil, and don't mind telling us so until we half believe it ourselves. Of course, all this Shanghai Club white superiority isn't entirely unselfish. They need it.

Life is usually quite a mess, and human beings are so little, so small. It does one good, therefore, to have a good ancestor and borrow a little of that reflected greatness. And if that is impossible, if not every one out here can show ancestral portraits in oil in his hall, it does one good also to believe that his primeval great-grandfather in the forest had the right blood in him. It sets everything right and engenders self-confidence, and self-confidence means success, as all American professors of psychology can tell you. And it relieves one of all desire to learn and study things Chinese. But I was talking about the origin of this inferiority complex and in particular was explaining where Miss Pan got her inferiority from. What with all this white superiority, and what with movie pictures of Mae West and Greta Garbo, the Chinese college girls are all but dying to have curly blonde hair and blue eyes. It never occurs to Miss Pan that a Chinese girl with straight, black hair and a slim, willowy figure could absolutely bewitch a European. The movie advertisements have done their work, the visible consequence of which is Miss Pan's proposed boycott against you when you dare to say that your ideal is Oriental beauty. Oriental beauty indeed! Why don't you discuss literature, but must discuss us poor girls?

You will undertsand now why, when you try to make the Chinese girls believe that they are charming and graceful and perhaps more dignified than their sisters in the West, the Chinese madonnas will just fling mud at you. You are not disheartened, are you? Meanwhile, go back to Paris and try to invent a formula for dyeing ladies' hair golden and ladies' eyes blue, and you will reap an enormous fortune in China with all the Chinese college girls as your ardent patron-admirers, besides receiving a warm welcome with big

banners by a delegation of Chinese college girls at the wharf
next time you come to China. They will then believe you are
serious.

Yours, etc.,

LIN YUTANG.

39

IN DEFENSE OF GOLD DIGGERS

ONE of the most curiously misunderstood classes in modern society are the so-called gold diggers. The existence of gold diggers is part and parcel of the present economic system, and under the present society, I think the gold diggers are merely women in a certain class who are more clear-minded than their sisters, being the female counterpart of "Big Business Brains," "realtors," bankers, and all the successful liars among men. Both the banker and the gold digger know what they want—money; both sell their goods to the highest bidders and both have no scruples about achieving their goal by the crookedest means. Moreover, I believe both have separate, water-tight compartments of ethics, their professional and their private morality.

A banker may be the gentlest of fathers and the kindest of friends, but in the execution of his professional duties, he would be a silly fool if he were to grow sentimental over driving a competitor out of business. All is fair in Big Business, and the man who can steal a march on his rival or crush him under his foot is very much respected for his superior business acumen and "executive ability." While I believe that a gold digger is out to get gold from the banker and his class and approaches that goal with the same sort of professional cynicism, I still think that she can be a very good daughter to her mother or a steadfast friend to her less fortunate and less able sisters.

It is necessary to establish the economic background of the gold digger before one can see this point clearly. It would be wrong, I think, to regard the gold diggers as the female counterpart of thieves and gangsters rather than of bankers among men, for the thieves have nothing to sell, while the gold diggers have—their sex.

Now a lot of confusion exists among men's minds about this matter of selling one's sex. One speaks of prostitutes as selling their sex, but it would be more proper and exact to speak of them as selling their bodies. Selling sex is a much more general affair. The mother who helps her débutante daughter to curl her hair before a ball in order to catch the eye of a young millionaire or English lord is as much selling her daughter's sex as the prostitute; and the department store manager who dismisses an old saleswoman to make place for a young, charming applicant is trying to sell her sex to his customers, in the strictest sense of the word, for the benefit of the shareholders. Her youth and her beauty, together with the powder and cream she is compelled to provide out of her own pocket, are part of the company's assets, acquired to develop the company's business. Our common notion of morality is that it is highly moral for a woman to sell her sex for the benefit of her employer until her youth and beauty are ground out of her by the daily routine of standing eight hours on high heels, but it is immoral for a woman to sell her sex directly and, here is the important point, to the disadvantage of men with a fat purse.

Our ideal of womanhood in this present industrial society is that a woman should achieve the highest feminine attraction at the lowest cost to men. If she is not expensive, men would not look at her, and if she is expensive, she is a gold digger. There comes a time when a clear-minded woman perceives this truth in her own intuitive manner, and decides that she should be consistently expensive, to men as well as to herself, before the depreciation in her assets descends to the zero point. This was the ugly thought of Victoria in W. L. George's *Bed of Roses,* who perceived that she was developing varicose veins as a restaurant waitress and injuring the beauty of her ankles.

Now, of course, men would prefer highly moral women who would caress them for nothing. All men like women who are sweet and charming and expect nothing from them. The ideal woman is one who abhors all thoughts of money. There are any number of such sweet young souls who would slave and save for their men and give their affection for a loyal heart in return. There are also any number of men who attend office, receive their pay, and obey the law. But it

is natural that there should be among both sexes people
who have a realistic sense of the importance of money, and
who make it their ambition in life to acquire as much wealth
as possible. Among the men they become bankers and "realtors," while among the women they become gold diggers,
for it is difficult to imagine what else they can do, except
marry a real-estate owner. They would, at any time, marry
a real-estate owner if they had a chance. While the real-
estate owner's wife rather looks down upon the gold digger
as the private ricksha puller looks down upon the tramp
ricksha coolie, I find it sometimes hard to look down upon
the tramp ricksha coolie because he pulls many men, and
look up to the private ricksha coolie because he pulls only
one. And who doesn't know that sometimes the private
coolie pulls also a good many men behind his employer's
back?

So I am quite willing to let all considerations of morality
alone. Even if the gold digger is a sinner, I will not cast the
first stone. What I am trying to say is that in both the bankers among men and the gold diggers among women there
rules essentially the same thought of deep wisdom that "those
who fail to provide for themselves will eventually injure
their friends and those who always provide for their friends
will eventually injure themselves," as Chang Ch'ao expressed
it in the seventeenth century. In them both, too, is cherished
the entirely human and laudable ambition of buying a villa
and retiring in comfort in their old age, without having to
"injure their friends" by sponging on them. Furthermore,
the banker, after having made enough money himself, proceeds to love and admire his wife who abhors all thoughts of
money, and the gold digger will eventually marry a poet and

bestow her caresses on him gratis. So what is there to choose between the two?

That is why I said that the gold diggers are merely more clear-minded than their sisters, just as the bankers are merely gifted with more hard sense than their fellow men. The banker and the gold digger, therefore, when they meet, should respect each other for their own clear-mindedness. If we admire a banker smoking a pipe in his comfortable armchair in his library of calf-bound books, why can't we be a little generous and admire the retired *grande dame* who smiles graciously at you under her glorious white hair from the window of her "Rose Cottage"? Who knows but she may have donated a few hospital beds, as so many Big Business Brains do?

40

SEX IMAGERY IN THE CHINESE LANGUAGE

THERE is sex imagery in every language, and the Chinese language is no exception. Without having made an exhaustive comparative study on the subject, I dare not make the statement that the Chinese language excels in this respect, but that would seem to be the general impression. The English miners' language and that of sailors on the forecastle could perhaps shame the Chinese by comparison, but I suspect nevertheless that such language is more confined to the forecastle and has less widespread currency. Speaking of the Amoy dialect, which alone I know intimately, I can easily trace certain expressions referring to *grand air, abject defeat,* or *ability* to definitely sexual imagery. The very common expression "Do you know a potato?" is beyond a doubt sexual in origin . . . but I see already we are delving into forbidden ground. I have not the standing of a Havelock Ellis to treat this subject without misunderstanding. . . . So I am afraid I have to confine myself entirely to another aspect of the problem, and discuss not the prevalence of terms with primary sexual meanings in Chinese, which would make everybody blush, but on the other hand discuss the amazing variety of perfectly harmless terms which have developed a secondary sexual meaning. I do not think any one need to blush at the term *clouds and rain,* which is one of the commonest literary expressions employed in this connection. The discussion will serve merely to illustrate euphemism in the sphere of sex, which solves the problem of taboo and enables Chinese novels to portray "imperative reticences" without offending the uninitiated.

Imagery from nature is the commonest used, and of this class, the *butterfly* and the *mandarin ducks* are perhaps the most frequently met with. One speaks of *mad bees drinking the nectar of flowers,* and of *mandarin ducks necking,* which is often given as a parallel expression for *phoenixes in a weird dance.* A less decidedly sexual image is contained in *trees with twin trunks* and *birds flying shoulder to shoulder,* which refer to great, devoted lovers. (This is after all not so bad as what is found in Shakespeare's *Othello* and *Romeo and Juliet.*)

Spring stands generally as a symbol of love, and carnal love especially. Thus we have expressions like *spring passion, spring mood* ("sexual passions, desires"), and *spring palace* (term for "pornography"). In this connection, it may be mentioned that the word *room* in the connection *room-business* is a perfectly respectable phrase referring to sexual acts, used for instance by doctors. Besides *spring,* the *wind,* and the *moon,* too, when used together, refer to sexual love.

Flower in Chinese is the symbol of girls and women, especially beautiful girls. To *hunt for flowers and inquire after willows* is to indulge in philandering with professional women. The world of sing-song girls is referred to as *the flower kingdom.* Venereal diseases are known in Chinese as *flower and willow diseases.* Then of course there are special references to certain flowers in particular connections. The *dew dropping in the opening peony flower* is decidedly obscene.

The phrase *clouds and rain* simply means "sexual intercourse" and is connected with a literary reference to the Wushan (Witches' Mountains) in the Yangtse Gorges, where the heaven joins the earth in an ever-changing world of clouds and mist. I strongly suspect that this is in some way connected with early phallic worship in Ch'u mythology.

Some modern words with new secondary obscene meanings are the *radio, injection,* and *electric bell.* I forbid myself mention of sex imagery from all walks of life found in folk songs. Suffice it to mention a few: the *water-pail in the well,* the *plot of land,* the *boatman,* the *monk,* etc.

It is strange, however, that sexual virility is referred to by the same word as that for "humanitarianism," *jentao.* Further, to know *human affairs* is to "reach puberty." The modern equivalent of the word "sex" is now *hsing* or "nature," a word which used to be very much belabored in Confucian philosophy. It is today the most general and respectable word of expressing "sex" in Chinese, as *hsingpieh* for "sexual distinctions," *hsingchiao* for "sexual intercourse," *hsingping* for "sexual diseases," and *hsing went'i* for "sexual problems."

41

THE MONKS OF HANGCHOW

I WENT to Hangchow in a fit. There are moments in our life when one feels the utter futility of the daily life we are leading, and must go somewhere, or else physically or mentally collapse. This feeling is variously called the "inner urge" for independence (by overfondled children), the "divine call" (by people going abroad for adventure among heathens), "religious duty" (by the Buddhist pilgrims), or "the subliminal uprush of the nomadic instinct" (by our professors of psychology). I call it more simply "the weather." Yes, it was the weather. I had to go somewhere.

We arrived on a rainy afternoon, and put up at the Lake-View Hotel. West Lake was never more beautiful, more poetic than on a day of spring showers, with clouds still nestling on its hillsides. As I stood before my window, I felt the air was filled with the fragrance of the moist spring, while the shower was so fine that one could only hear its soft, silent drizzle, invisible like the passing of angels' footsteps, on the tree leaves and the blades of grass and the wet earth. Here and there, in the foreground, were farmers' huts, surrounded with trees and verdure in such a generous measure that one could weep to think of the Shanghai bankers' homes, and wonder why one must be worth a quarter million in order to own a pitiful acre of rolled, mown, and enclosed lawn, atrociously decorated with a few geometric flowerbeds, resembling the blocks that children play with.

When at Hangchow, I always went to see the fish of Yu-chuan in a pond of transparent water, built around a spring. These fish were dignified beings, and some of them, according to the polite and good-mannered monk I was talking with, were fifty or sixty years old. When they become old invalids, then their skin, which is normally dark blue, turns gray, like old people's hair; they develop digestive troubles, dislike movement, and then one day pop off from this earthly life. The monk said they always gave them a decent burial.

"As vegetarians, do you eat eggs?" I asked.

"We don't," he answered in Honan dialect. "But why shouldn't we really, so long as they have not been fertilized? Here we don't, but the monks at Tienchu eat meat, and even marry and have children."

The conversation was getting interesting. I thought that whatever might be said about the virtues of the vegetarian diet, I had never seen a healthy rosy-complexioned monk. I could not help asking if the vegetarian food was not necessary for their celibate life.

The monk was too cultured to answer that question in the presence of the ladies, so I asked the latter to study the fish from the other corner, and we were soon deep in the modern marriage problem. The monk's evident sincerity invited the discussion.

"Take that girl, for instance. Are you not subject to her sex appeal?"

In reply to this rather crude question, the monk gave me one of the best sermons on the single life I have ever heard. It all amounts to about the same thing as Plato's dictum that philosophers should never marry.

"Of course, I am aware of her charm. But I am also aware of its consequences. How many young men are committing suicide every day, and all for what? For love! For women!" He was getting as cynical as the author of Ecclesiastes. "Why is it that there are so many divorces? Divorce means that you want to get rid of the woman without whom you thought you could not live some years ago. Look at me! I can go to Taishan or Miaofengshan, Putu or Swatow, whenever I choose to. I am a free man!"

I discovered that here was a fellow spirit of St. Paul, Immanuel Kant, and Samuel Butler. In fact, I was drinking at the very fountain where Schopenhauer had got all his wisdom about women. He advised me to study the Buddhist classics. Some confessions about the technique of sex-repression (like the double-crossing of legs), and worse confessions about its failure, must necessarily be kept confidential and passed over lightly here as things of no consequence, if the Little Critic is to remain respectable. . . .

Next morning, we hired a car for a trip to Hupao. Passing along the Suti, we got a most wonderful view of the lake, newly bathed in the April showers. Magic islands covered with tall, green trees seem to spring out of the water, and cast reflections as still as themselves. Only a hideous structure of the lighthouse type stands out against this beautiful landscape, like a ringworm sore on a beauty's face. I asked the chauffeur what it was, and was told it was the West Lake Exposition Memorial. It was difficult to imagine anything quite so shameless, and I decided that if I should ever lead an army and capture Hangchow, my first duty would be to aim a howitzer against this skin disease on Hsihu's surface and wipe it off the face of the earth.

The walk leading to the temple at Hupao was one of the most satisfying to be found in the neighborhood of Hsihu. While gazing at the rivulet rushing down by the side of the mountain path, I saw a father trying vainly to get his young daughter of six to approach the rivulet, where there was a toy waterfall. The girl didn't want to see the waterfall. It would make her shoes wet. She disclaimed all interest in the waterfall. I was then convinced that China had really gone to the dogs.

Hupao is famous for its tea, and I have heard some people come from miles away to drink tea at Hupao. I was, however, more attracted by its teakettle. Maybe such kettles have existed elsewhere in China, but I had not seen them before. It was undoubtedly a most ingenious invention, a product of monastic leisure. Western monks have made superb wine, so why shouldn't the Hupao monks invent a superb kettle. It was made of brass and shaped like the ordinary round kitchen kettles, handle, spout, and all, but of an unusual size, about two feet high and two and half across in diameter. The body itself was a combination of water tank and oven, with coals fed from underneath, and two scientific-looking funnels on top. The handle was merely decorative, but there was a regular spout, although it was unimaginable how any one could pour water from it. I asked for a demonstration. The monk took a can, poured some spring water down one of the funnels, and instantaneously boiling water overflew from its spout. The monk was already holding the can against it to receive the boiling water. The operation was extremely simple and easy. I was fully conscious of the principles of physics involved in it, but was too ashamed to mention scientific terms to him. And it had the great advantage of keeping the pot full and boiling all the time. If governments had as much wisdom as the monk who invented this kettle, and would put in as much as they take out of the people every time, oh, well ...

On the top of the Hupao temple was the Chikung pagoda, memorial to a famous old Buddhist priest. The inscription said that on the day of his death, Chikung appeared at Yuyao, and delivered a pair of sandals (at the time they had already been cremated with Chikung's body), which were identified as his old sandals by his fellow priests. On the same day, he appeared also at Liuho pagoda miles away and delivered a letter to a fellow priest, which was recognized as in his own handwriting. Now, these were the stories of contemporary eye witnesses, and should have been incorporated in the "Evidences of Buddhistianity" like many stories of the "Acts of the Apostles." It should be remarked here parenthetically that, although a local saint, Chikung went about healing people and performed miraculous cures, so that quite a legend had grown up soon after his death, as recorded in the popular novel *Life of Chikung,* running to twice the length of the *Red Chamber Dream*. I still remember how it was told in this novel that Chikung was one day performing a cure on a six-year-old child. He said the medicine required was common enough, but it should be taken with the tears of a man fifty-two years old, born on the fifth day of the fifth moon, mixed with those of a girl of nineteen, born on the fifth day of the eighth moon. I forget whether these tears were ultimately found or not, but these were the stories of eyewitnesses who saw Chikung in the flesh before he died and appeared once at Yuyao and a second time at Liu pagoda to some of his favorite disciples.

42

THE MONKS OF TIENMU

IT IS my principle, when visiting a temple, to act as a detective and find out all the sins of the monks. From childhood on, I have read and heard stories about monks and nuns as seducers of girls and young men, for monks are made fun of in Chinese stories as they are in Boccaccio's tales. I ascribe the popularity of this sort of story to the ultimate desire of mankind to see sham and hypocrisy exposed. I have listened to tales of nuns keeping young men in a special room for months, and to other stories describing the monks of various temples as keeping women by the scores in an underground cellar. Actually, however, I think the monks have been given greater credit than is their due, although at different periods in Chinese history, under the reign of Ch'enghua, for example, in the Ming Dynasty monasteries were made use of as hotbeds for seditious activities, and when monasteries began to house boxers and politicians, it was not improbable that they should house a few women in the cellars as well. But on the whole, from my observation, most monks are too anemic and too underfed to be capable of such Don Juan exploits as the popular stories ascribe to their credit. Besides the innate desire of mankind to get even with people professing better lives than ourselves, there is a further aesthetic reason for placing a lurid story in a religious background for the purpose of intriguing men's imagination and enhancing its artistic effect.

Naturally there are no cellars containing women in the S——, which is more a monastery than a temple, at the West Tienmu Mountains, where I spent part of a summer vacation. It took a few days for me to satisfy myself on this point, for this is a monastery housing over a hundred monks and capable of accommodating from seven to eight hundred pilgrims. So many courtyards are forbidden ground, and there are so many closed doors. I peeped at every crevice, went to the end of every blind alley with a closed door, and ventured into the sacred ground of the retired abbots' quarters. I surveyed every low wall, scanned every underground structure, and bribed my way into every closed courtyard, before arriving at the conclusion after a few days that I was an utter fool. There were still great possibilities, but I was convinced there were no cellars containing women in them.

I succeeded, however, in coming to understand the character of Chinese monks and the inner life of a Chinese monastery. If I did not find the monks to be downright immoral, I came to see them as ordinary human beings. What politics were going on here in this haven of peace and what excitement! There had been fights, the abbot had run away, after escaping by jumping down from the veranda, and no one had been found willing to take up the onerous position of an abbot—except one who consented merely to act in a temporary capacity. It was almost as bad as Tsinan University itself!

Like all good detectives, I work with young children. I found an intelligent and sweet-looking lad of fourteen who came to chat with me, while I was catching shrimps with my bare hands for my children in a mountain brook by the temple. We got on well. He was working for the monastery. I gave him two cigarettes and we became fast friends. He smoked one and kept the other. The following day, he told me that some monks had tried to get the extra cigarette from him, but he had refused. From him I got more inside stories of the monks than I could get from any grown-up, and I suspect I knew things which had escaped the eyes of the abbot. I knew, for instance, which one of the monks ate meat on the sly in a dark room in the restaurant near by and which one didn't. And when the boy told me that such-and-such a monk was a real vegetarian, I was ready to believe that he was a real vegetarian. The percentage of real vegetarians seemed, according to his report, alarmingly small, but I will be generous, besides being generally incredulous whenever Chinese try to give figures.

About women, the monks were no worse and no better than the outside world. The boy told me cases to convince me they were normal human beings. But we will leave them and their women alone and talk of monkish politics.

Little did I realize the undercurrents of politics when I arrived at the Temple. Outwardly it was a haven of rest and peace, and it was, so far as the tourists were concerned. But before I arrived, there had been a bloody fight between two opposite factions, one trying to drive the abbot out. The abbot was attacked in his own living rooms and, being a husky fellow, jumped from a veranda twelve feet from the ground. A few of his brethren were badly mauled and were in a hospital in Hangchow.

Three days later, I saw some six peasants pretending to weed the garden below our rooms. This seemed rather strange. Soon soldiers appeared outside the wall and blocked the side gate. Their chief summoned the peasants to follow him into another part of the monastery. Very soon it was reported five monks had been arrested for smoking opium. What happened was, these were the remaining ringleaders of the opposition party, and the fact of smoking opium was merely an excuse for calling in soldiers and purging the temple of their seditious influence by handing them over to the police.

So I am led to believe there is always enough plot for a novel wherever human beings gather together, provided one takes the trouble to find out the mental life of the people, be it in a monastery or a hospital or a convent school. What jealousy, what passion, and what romance! Any one going through the spick-and-span corridors of a modern hospital, where cleanliness and orderliness reign supreme, would hardly suspect that an exciting and intensely human drama is always being enacted among the doctors and nurses—so full of professional jealousy and human ambition and furtive love and selfless devotion and heroic sacrifice and sometimes tragic sorrow. Lately, so many movie stories and novels have been based on love in a hospital that there is no reason another might not be written with a monastery as the background. As I write, the abbot has returned from Hangchow, having been told that the ringleaders have been rounded up, and with him some of his faithful friars, two of them still wearing patches of antiseptic cotton and gauze on their faces.

43

A TALK WITH BERNARD SHAW

BERNARD SHAW once looked in at Shanghai and looked out again. On the morning of his arrival, the papers reported that the local Rotary Club had decided to snub Shaw by letting him "pass unnoticed." The apparent implication was, of course, that Shaw would suffer such terrible disgrace from being passed unnoticed by the local Rotarians that he would never be able to recover his reputation. That was, of course, very intelligent on the part of the Shanghai Rotarians in view of the fact that the Hong Kong Rotarians had been worse than snubbed by Bernard Shaw. But it would have been still more intelligent to decide not to read Shaw altogether. Shaw had aroused, besides, such a scare among the Shanghai respectable society by urging the Hong Kong students to study communism that the entire Shanghai foreign press was in hiding that morning for fear of coming into contact with him. The attitude of the Rotary Club was but typical. The only thing, however, that will go down to posterity about the Shanghai Rotary Club is that on the day preceding Shaw's arrival, these Rotarians, or by Shaw's definition, these people who "keep in the rut," called Shaw "Blighter," "Ignoramus," "Fa Tz" and "Bakayaro." However, the best fun is still to be had, if Sinclair Lewis will pass through Shanghai some day, and the Shanghai Rotary Club will be really ignorant enough as to invite the author of *Babbitt* to luncheon, as they most probably will, if they haven't read the book. The Babbitts of this small town can then absolutely do nothing else than use more international invectives like "Blighter," "Fa Tz" and "Bakayaro," and they will then have the historic distinction of snubbing two Nobel Prize Winners.

It was tiffin hour in Madame Sun Yat-sen's parlor. Shaw was sitting in an armchair by the fireside, gazing off and on at the fire, perfectly at ease and in the best of health. One noticed the small light blue eyes, whose light reflected the quizzical, diabolical ideas that were dashing about and playing pranks inside his Mephistophelean forehead. When an Englishman sits by the fire, he is just himself, and so was Shaw. Dr. Tsai and Madame Sun were in the room, but a few other guests had not yet arrived, so we talked at random.

The conversation turned to Shaw's biographers. I suggested that Frank Harris was much more readable than Henderson.

"Readable, yes," Shaw said. "But Harris was a perfectly impossible man. He was destitute, so he wanted to write a life of Jesus. His publisher would have none of it, and suggested that he write a life of Bernard Shaw. That was the origin of it. But he knew nothing about me. He got his facts all wrong. Before he had quite got through with his manuscripts, Harris died, leaving them in my care. I had to take three months to edit, correct, and supply the facts, while leaving the opinions as they stand."

"Harris mentioned that he found the subject of Jesus too overpowering for him," I essayed, merely to show that I had read the book.

"Yes, Harris would talk about the beauty of the character of Jesus, when he found himself in a debauchee company, but when you put him in the company of Anglican priests, he would talk—eh—as if he were conversing with the most abandoned Parisian cocotte." I noticed the pause, because I remembered he had said about the same thing in his Postscript to Harris's work, the difference being that, instead of using the analogy of the "abandoned Parisian cocotte," he said in the book that if Harris "took in a quiet deaconess he would entertain her on the assumption that her personal morals and religious views were those of our postwar nightclubs."

"When he died, he left his wife not a penny." Shaw went on.

"I hope his wife is getting all the royalties from his book, although you had to write a great part of it," I said.

"Of course," Shaw replied, "the amusing thing is, some

of my friends have written to me protesting against my leaving in the offensive things he said about me, which he shouldn't have said. As a matter of fact, these passages were written by myself."

While he was talking, his light blue eyes blinked occasionally against the light, which gave the impression that he was a highly sensitive soul, by no means incapable of shyness. His most characteristic expression was undoubtedly the knitting of his brows, which gave them that diabolical slant, so familiar in the Chinese theatrical masks of ghosts and wicked generals and generally so well portrayed in cartoons of Shaw—a slant which was comfortably relieved by a paradoxical grin hidden somewhere beneath his bushy white beard.

Here was this tall, lanky Irish thinker who had frightened many people by his unholy and highly un-Christian habit of telling the truth in the most forcible manner in his writings, and yet who was so human, affable, natural, who belonged as much to our human world as the gray tweed suit he wore. The world would not believe that Shaw shocked the world simply because he was strictly observing the Eighth Commandment (anyway, that one about not lying), which our Christian ethics and social conventions have forbidden the Christians from following. Anybody who will speak the truth about society is bound to shock the world. The characteristic of Shaw, as it is in fact of all true humorists, is that he possesses more hard, honest common sense than other men in his thinking, the same common sense which makes him so truly human, courteous, and affable in his personal relations, in spite of his Mephistophelean appearance.

I was entrusted with the duty of asking Madame Sun to loan G.B.S. to the Pen Club for twenty minutes. When the subject was mentioned, Shaw said:

"I should like to oblige, but you know I might be compelled to speak. You know I went to the Hong Kong University with the determination not to speak, and when I was there, the students shouted '—We—want—Bernard—Shaw' until I had to give in. Well, you know the results." He was referring to the Hong Kong Rotarians' chagrin. "I am a member of the Pen Club myself, you know. When Galsworthy wanted me to join, I promised to become a life member, which simply means paying more membership fees than the ordinary members, on the condition that I was not to hear anything more about it."

However, with some persuasion, Shaw, with his characteristic courtesy, accepted the invitation.

At tiffin, which was vegetarian, Shaw talked about vegetarianism, the Chinese family system, the war, the teaching of drama in English universities, Chinese tea, and Instant Postum. Shaw was just talking, when he was not eating or managing his chop sticks, but Shavian wisdom dropped upon the air for whosoever had the ear to catch it.

After tiffin, the party went out into the garden. The afternoon sun was shining gloriously upon Shaw's white head and tall figure. It was unusual, at least at this time of the year for Shanghai, and one could not help thinking that Shaw was getting a better impression of the Shanghai sky than it deserved.

"You are lucky to see the sun in Shanghai," someone had said.

"Oh, really it is nothing," I interrupted. "The sun shone in

Shanghai once in 1905, and then again in 1923." I was trying to be historical.

"No, it is the sun that is lucky to see Bernard Shaw in Shanghai," replied the Irish wit.

I thought of Mohammed and the Mountain.

44

A SUGGESTION FOR SUMMER READING

WHEN the atmosphere is hovering around one hundred degrees, it is entirely natural and human that our thoughts should turn to summer resorts, waterfalls, pine forests and swimming suits. It is also natural that one should cast about for some kind of an "omnibus" that one can take along to the resort for whiling away the hours under the cool shade of a pine forest or on the brink of a gurgling stream.

The difficulty of choosing books for summer reading is that our requirements vary with our moods, and as it is apparently impossible to take a whole suitcase of books, it is rather difficult to set one's choice upon a single volume that will answer the varying moods of the reader. Of course, a novel is the natural thing, but with a novel one often has the uncomfortable feeling of fear, as one draws toward the end, of what one is going to do with oneself next week when it is finished. Also the summer heat is not conducive to such long, continued reading. Like the books that one puts on the bedside table, it should not be so fascinating as to prevent you from going to sleep.

A good book for summer reading, as well as for the bedside table, should be one like Boswell's *Life of Johnson,* which is both light and informative and which one can begin reading at any page and leave off at any page when overcome by drowsiness. It should, furthermore, not be confined to any one field, but should contain a fund of information on the most varied topics. For all these reasons, I am sincerely recommending a dictionary.

There is one such dictionary in the English language which, as many reviewers have pointed out, is good not only for reference, but for general reading as well. This is the *Pocket Oxford Dictionary of Current English,* a little marvel of condensation which compels the more wonder and admiration the longer one uses it.

Imagine turning up the little volume, which occupies no more space than two pairs of stockings, and coming upon such delights as await one under the word "horse." I don't think anybody could be so weary of life that he could not find absorbing interest in that article and get a certain amount of thrill from the following phrases: "flog a dead horse," "grin through a horse's collar" (practice elementary humor), "look a gift horse in the mouth," "mount a high horse," "eat, work, like a horse." It will be also interesting to learn the exact meaning of "horse flesh" and "horse marines" ("tell that to the horse marines"), and to note the way in which "horse-leech" is used in the English language ("daughters of the horse-leech," Prov. XXX. 15); also "horse latitudes" (belt of calms at northern edge of N.E. trade-winds). For myself I am most delighted by the phrases "horse laugh" and "horse play"; I find "horse sense" is not here, but should be—is it possible that this is a purely American idiom? We usually talk a language so limited by an anemic, stale, overused vocabulary, that it is refreshing to be reminded of the existence of words like "horse sense" and "horse laugh."

I realize that perhaps the pleasure that I derive from the *Pocket Oxford Dictionary* is that of a Chinese student of English, but I do not think this tells the whole story. Every man gifted with a fine sense of the shades of meaning of words should be interested in examining the way in which the common words of his mother tongue are tumbled about in everyday conversation. I grant that the pleasure is perhaps keener for a Chinese student, and from this standpoint, I think any Englishman would derive an equally great pleasure from studying a Chinese dictionary, if there was one compiled on the same principles as the P.O.D. Imagine his delight when he comes upon such a turn of expression in a Chinese dictionary as "he talks like aerated water" and "we went through mountain paths that resembled a sheep's intestines," "if one asks for death, one cannot die; and if one asks for life, one cannot live." Who would not be impressed by the concrete imagery of the Chinese language when he finds the question "Am I a hookworm in his belly?" as a current expression equivalent in meaning to the English "How could I know what is in his mind?" Or who would not be impressed by the terseness of the Chinese language when he finds that, when an Englishman takes about twenty or thirty words to express the thought that "If you stay idle at your home and eat and do nothing, even a family fortune as big as a mountain will vanish," the Chinese expresses it only by the four words, "Sit, eat, mountain empty"?

Take the Chinese word "horse" for example. One would find under the word *ma,* or horse, such phrases as "firing crackers at a horse's buttocks," which is an expression referring to taking a sly fatal dig at a person toward the end of an essay after long paragraphs of apparent eulogy, or giving public demonstration against a public official when he is leaving office. We have also phrases like "don't be an ox or a horse for your children and grandchildren," which is advice to old men against slaving for money in order to build up fortunes which will be squandered by their children soon after their death. Other phrases, for example, are, "I will only look at your horse's head" (I will follow your banner wherever you go); "horse's teeth are already long" (a man is already too old); "my whip, however long, cannot reach the horse's belly" (the matter is beyond my control); "the anti-social horse" (black sheep), and so forth.

One could delve into the regions of folk psychology by a comparison of the different ways in which words are handled in colloquial and literary idioms by different nations. One could, for instance, learn from the Chinese use of the word for "intestines" or "belly" an important psychological trait of the Chinese people. While these words are taboo in English and reveal the prudery of the English-speaking people, they count among the most poetic words of the Chinese language. The theory of poetic diction which Wordsworth put forth about using simple everyday words in poetry, was never carried out by Wordsworth himself to the same extent as by the Chinese poets. Among other aspects of Chinese literature, we have very few taboos in Chinese, for we are so in love with this earthly life that we regard nothing as too low or trivial to go into poetry. Take for instance the verse that I saw once on the wall of a Hangchow restaurant:

> The bamboo shoots are fresh and I find my rice-bowl too small;
> The fish is delicious and my intestines are broadened for wine.

What American poet would dare to incorporate ham and sweet potatoes into his verse or sing about the condition of his alimentary canal?

From the use of the word "belly," one finds that the Chinese think much more emotionally than the Europeans, for the belly is for us the seat of all our thoughts, feelings, scholarship, and learning, as may be seen from the phrases "a bellyful of literature," "a bellyful of scholarship," "a bellyful of sorrow"—which come very near to the English use of "bowels" in the biblical sense. Now modern psychologists have established the fact that the intestines are the seat of our emotions such as fear, anger, hatred, and sorrow, which are all generated through certain secretions circulating in our intestines and our veins. Without any knowledge of ductless glands or other discoveries of modern psychology, the Chinese feels instinctively that his sorrow originates below his diaphragm; for instance, from the fact that one loses all appetite in times of great sorrow. The mechanism of the internal organs has, we feel, apparently been disturbed.

This corroborates my theory about the femininity of Chinese thinking, for the Chinese think like women. Isadora Duncan said very wisely "Women's thoughts originate in the abdomen and travel upwards, while men's thoughts originate in the head and travel downwards," and I am quite sure the thoughts of the Chinese originate below the diaphragm, as all women's do. It is therefore true that the more emotional our type of thinking is, the more are the intestines responsible for our thinking. In fact, I have no doubt that the Chinese are such great poets because they think with their intestines. Whereas an Englishman says that he "ransacks his brains" for ideas, we say that a man "ransacks his dried intestines" for lines of poetry.

Such is the fun one can get out of reading a dictionary. Whole categories of words may be singled out at random. For instance, one can make the amazing discovery that the word "stupidity" to a Chinese connotes an entirely different meaning from what it does in English. A man may call himself "keeper of stupidity" and call his studio "the stupidity hut," and an old cypress tree with bare rugged branches may be described by the word "stupid," by which one means that it has a kind of strange, antique beauty. One finds that words denoting "sickness," "thinness," "laziness," and "listlessness" are among the words most commonly used in Chinese poetry. I do not suggest that there is such a Chinese dictionary to be had at present, but I strongly believe that such a work should occupy the loving labor of some scholar who has not lost his sense of the magic of words.

45

THE 500TH ANNIVERSARY OF PRINTING

ON THE 500th anniversary of the invention of printing in Europe, few would dispute the debt we owe to Gutenberg. It would be insane for any one to argue against the inestimable benefits printing confers upon our daily life. The whole intellectual character of the modern age is made possible by the devices of quickly multiplying knowledge and making it available to the common man. Moreover, true progress of civilization must be measured by the availability of increased knowledge and its new benefits to the common man.

It may be safely assumed that on this point every one is agreed. It may further be assumed that there is no going back to the bliss of ignorance and general illiteracy of medieval days. What I wish to point out is rather the fact that, like all good things in life, printing has raised new problems in our daily mental life the solution of which calls for our greatest effort and wisdom.

Having made my general position clear, I may at once point out a situation which has arisen as a result of all modern developments following upon the invention of printing, the quick multiplication of knowledge, and the mass of scientific and general information confronting us today, which is fast becoming unmanageable. The problem is how this situation, coupled with the cheapness of reading material, has affected the mental life of the average individual— the content of his mind, his mental relationship to the world around him, and ultimately the character of his reading and thinking.

It would be extremely hazardous to assume too readily that in these three respects the modern man is decidedly better off. We now can hardly conceive an intellectual life without printed books and newspapers. Yet it is a healthy thought to remember that Shakespeare certainly did not possess a single English dictionary and read fewer books per week than the modern regular customer of the rental library.

One must first admit that here a problem exists for the average individual. From the point of view of the average newspaper and book reader, modern man's knowledge has undoubtedly increased in scope. The real question is whether the material of knowledge is better or worse assimilated, or whether piecemeal information has not increased at the expense of real comprehension. There is evidently a limit to our capacity for assimilated knowledge. Meanwhile the growing mass of knowledge has so rapidly multiplied that I believe assimilation can no longer keep pace with knowledge, to the detriment of our intellectual well-being. Modern man is more widely read, but he is also more confused, more perplexed, and on the whole knows less what to think of the world around him. He does not even know what to read, simply because he has too much to read, and ends up generally by reading more promiscuously than the medieval scholar before Gutenberg's day.

It would be interesting to compare the mental state of the modern scholar with that of the ancient scholar. There were ancient scholars who knew all there was to know in the books—in the classics, poetry, history, philosophy, and what bits of physics and astronomy there were in their day—and felt fine, because in them there was a sense of mastery, a unification of human knowledge in one person. In a true sense, they were masters, and the word "teacher" was a term of great honor. Knowledge was integrated.

The situation of the modern scholar is decidedly less comfortable, and what is bad for the scholar cannot be good for the world in general. Today the mass of available knowledge has grown to formidable, unwieldy proportions, no longer encompassable by a single human mind. The rapid multiplication of books, coupled with the tendency toward overspecialization, has brought us to an intellectual impasse that must sooner or later be recognized as a world problem.

The invention of printing has done more to change the content of the average man's mind than anything else. That content is one of the most curious and terrifying phenomena of the modern age. We know too much and too little. We all have a mass of information and opinions on world-wide topics, from Hitler's schizophrenia to Mussolini's daughter, from the rise of Kemal Pasha to the proper breeding of turkeys. And yet we really know very little on these subjects. What's in our minds resembles what's in the town gossip's, widened to cover the world. It is as if we were looking at a remote landscape through a field glass that brings just enough details to justify all sorts of exciting speculations. We are all suffering from a surfeit of undigested information, and all floating blissfully on the surface of imaginary and rather undependable, borrowed opinions. Nobody knows anything any more. The more I read the more ignorant I become. The choice today before any educated man is between unread innocence and well-read ignorance.

Evidently, the end of human culture is that the educated, thinking man shall have an intelligent understanding of what is happening around him and that he himself shall remain an integrated personality. As the situation stands today, the man of 1940 comprehends less of what is happening around him than the man of 1450 in Europe or the man of 1740 in China. This is not the fault of printing, but of the complications of modern life. Of course, quantitatively, the modern man, by all odds, knows more things, but in relation to the world around him indubitably he knows less.

The phrase "the world around him" must be defined as the world to which he bears a vital relationship, the world which influences his life and which he therefore needs to comprehend. The medieval man knew less, but his world was easier to comprehend and he was intellectually more comfortable. Now, while the modern man actually has more piecemeal information, the world around him has also grown enormously complex. Human problems have grown to superhuman proportions, too big for the average mind, even for the superior mind.

It is possible to maintain with some show of correctness that today printing kills reading and reading kills thinking. According to Schopenhauer, too much reading directly inhibits our own active, individual thinking. "The constant streaming in of the thoughts of others must confine and suppress our own and indeed in the long run paralyze the power of thought. . . . When we read, another person thinks for us. . . . So it comes about that if any one spends almost the whole day in reading . . . he gradually loses the capacity for thinking."

Having read somewhat promiscuously on geographically remote subjects upon which it is impossible for us to check up personally, we naturally sift and patch up and make a guess as to the truth. It is undoubtedly in some such manner that individual opinion in a modern literate democracy is made up. Eventually we reject what we do not like to believe and label it propaganda or counter-propaganda and arrive at true ignorance, which is a state of not knowing that we do not know.

What is the remedy? The answer is certainly not to stop printing or stop reading, but more and better reading. A reasonable answer, I think, would be to give more thought to the problem of the average man's reading, to furnish better guides to reading, and to achieve a more definite ideal of the all-around man in our college education. Finally, the art of reading has to be better understood.

There are no panaceas even for intellectual evils. But concrete steps can be and have been taken in this direction. In the field of college education Columbia University already has arranged for all its freshmen to read certain great classics in the original, and not through "histories," and "outline" courses. What is being done at St. John's College at Annapolis, where students are required to read in four years' time the hundred most important epoch-making books in the history of human thought seems to be an admirable effort to achieve a unified view of human knowledge in all its aspects for the college student.

What surprises me most is the absence of a good guide to reading for the private reader, a situation which arises out of an unwieldy mass of publications. Good public libraries have librarians who give competent advice, but a handy guide for one's private library is definitely lacking. Such a selective guide in a few hundred to a thousand words for one subject (say, the U.S.S.R.) might give concise indications as to the nature of the books listed. This kind of literary guide has been compiled in Germany in the one-volume *Literarischer Ratgaber* by the Duererbund.

These may be brilliant or stupid ideas. But the reality of the problem of the average man's reading cannot be ignored.

46

BASIC ENGLISH AND PIDGIN

WHEN George III was ruling England and refused to learn to speak English correctly, he little dreamed that the English language was to become, in the space of a hundred fifty years, the common language of international intercourse for the modern world. Nor probably did he suspect that the language would be so altered that in 1923, H. L. Mencken could accuse him (in his "Declaration of American Independence" in American Vulgate) of making "the Legislature meet at one-horse tank-towns out in the alfalfa belt," or "getting the judges under his thumb by turning them out when they done anything he didn't like, or holding up their salaries, so that they had to cough up or not get no money," or "every time he has went to work and pulled any of these things, we have went to work and put in a kick, but every time we have went to work and put in a kick he has went to work and did it again!" The fact is, George III, by his insolence in refusing to talk English, has brought about the American independence and greatly helped the spread of the English language, while the English and Americans, by their insolence in refusing to speak any other tongue, have made it into the inevitable international language of today.

For the English are a strange people. Without any plan or purpose, they have created a working international language. If English has become the international tongue, the English could not give any reasons for it. It was rather a German philologist the great Jacob Grimm, a "boche" contemporary of George III, who prophesied that English some day would become the international language, because "in wealth, wisdom and strict economy, none of the other living languages can vie with it." The English have not wanted to create a world medium; they have nevertheless done so by simply refusing to be "bothered" with any other tongue. When an Englishman orders a cup of beef tea and gets a beef steak in a French restaurant, it is understood the French waiter owes him an apology for not knowing the English tongue, but when Taine ordered a beef steak and got a cup of beef tea in London, the fault lay, of course, entirely with Taine. That is how the English language has become the inevitable international tongue.

The fact remains, however, that English has become the language for international commercial and social intercourse, especially in the East, with the exception of Japan. When the Japanese begin to talk English as a nation, we may be sure something must be wrong either with the English language or with the Japanese. Apart, however, from the Japanese, none of whom I have ever known to talk English well, this language has clearly established its ascendancy over other languages in the world. Linguistic history teaches us that once a dialect or language has established its ascendancy over the others and thus gained a certain currency and prestige, it has every chance of steadily increasing its influence, as in the case of the London dialect which is the lineal ancestor of modern English or the Parisian dialect, which stands in the same relation to modern French. The same tendency ought to work in the case of an international language. Against the constantly spreading influence of English, powerfully aided by the radio and the talkies, artificial creations like Esperanto, Ido, and Novial seem to stand a very small chance.

There have been conscious attempts to remove certain difficulties which stand in the way of adoption of English as a medium of international intercourse. Reforms in grammar are the least important. Modern English has practically done away with the philologically inexplicable gender, except in the third person singular; the illogical and highly inconvenient "whom" is already fast disappearing in educated English ("Who is it from?" "Who to?"); the monosyllabic "don't" (current already in Columbia University lecture rooms) will before long supplant the bisyllabic "doesn't" for obvious reasons. James Joyce and pidgin English will do the rest and complete that historical process until English is as simple and as logical as Chinese.

Of reforms in spelling, with a conscious view to making English an international medium, the "Anglic" invented by Professor Zachrisson of Upsala is perhaps most worthy of attention. It has already the support or approval of eminent authorities like Daniel Jones of London University. Bewildered by the current phonetic marks, the English do not know that English spelling could be made amazingly simple: the long vowels (with "r" combinations), the short vowels, and "ah," "ow," "aw," "oi," "er," the long and short "oo's" and an unaccented vowel could cover all the English vowel sounds. "Anglic" writes the long sounds as "ae," "ee," "ie," "oe," "ue," and leaves the short vowels as they are. It is a system that could be read by anyone without any previous acquaintance, and its spelling is strictly scientific and much more accurate than Standard English.

"Basic English," started by C. K. Ogden, approached the problem from a new angle by limiting the basic vocabulary to be learned for international use to eight hundred fifty words. The idea is to have a mnemonic list of words which could be put on the back of a letter paper and memorized, words which are not subject to violently irregular declensions, and which will cover the bare needs of general intercourse without claims to literary beauty. Of these eight hundred fifty, the first hundred consist of "operators," including eighteen verbs and words like "if, because, so, as, just, only, but, to, for, through, yes, no," etc. There are four hundred "general names" like "copper, cork, copy, cook, cotton," and two hundred "common things" or "picturables" like "cake, camera, card, cart, cat," and one hundred and fifty "qualifiers" or adjectives, like "common, complex, conscious." The unique thing is that there are no verbs except the eighteen among the operators: "come, get, give, go, keep, let, make, put, seem, take, be, do, have, say, see, send, may, will." These with the three pronouns "I, you, he" are conjugated in full. We find, however, words denoting actions among the "necessary names" such as "reading, writing, knowledge, talk, thought, run, look, cry, cough, sleep, sneeze." About three hundred words are formed from these necessary names by adding *-ing* or *-ed*. (A word like "based" from "base" is, therefore, possible in Basic.) Numerals, measurements, names of currency and the calendar are not included, nor are proper names, but these could be learned separately. A further hundred and fifty words may be added for scientific reading material, making the total one thousand. It is claimed that these words suffice for general use, that words not in the list could all be circumlocuted, and that students may learn new words by having them explained by the basic vocabulary.

There is no question of the essential value of such a wise selection of vocabulary for people who must get along with what they have time for and who do not aspire to go into the niceties of the English language. It must be remembered, however, that the idiomatic use of these eight hundred and fifty words is something quite different from memorizing their meaning on the list. But the students at least have the advantage of readily understanding correspondence or books written in Basic English, when they have mastered the vocabulary. Idioms and turns of expression will have to be construed largely from the context. The gradual atrophy of English declensional forms and the highly analytic character of modern English (thus coming among the European languages nearest the Chinese) have made such a limitation of material possible. Few people realize that "going to" has largely supplanted "will" or "shall" (not in Basic) for the future, and "have to" with a perfect conjugation ("had to," "have to," and "will have to") is commonly used to replace "must" (not in Basic) which is defective for the past. "Look up to" could serve for "respect" and "look down upon" for "despise." The same analytic character is also seen in "look over" a lesson, "look into" a company's accounts, "look upon" something as so-and-so, "look back" at past experience, etc. This analytic and already highly monosyllabic character of spoken English may be illustrated in the following (American) sentence: "What a guy wants is a lot of push and grit that will keep him on the go and not see red or fall flat and get scared when someone shoots a pop-gun at you." Dorothy Dix is full of these short words.

For instance, quoting Lou Gehrig: " 'I'm not a guy to pop off and claim that I'll do this or that. I'm doing the best I can. If it isn't good enough, McCarthy will get me out of there. If it is, then I'll stick. I feel fine. So far as I know, I haven't changed my style at bat. I just don't hit in the spring, that's all. And as you get older, it takes longer to get into the swing of things. I'd like to help you and say something, but what can I say?' "

A more important question is the choice of this basic vocabulary. Precisely because English has this highly idiomatic character, it seems that it will lose a great deal, when in the choice of vocabulary, the emphasis is laid on the less changeable, but more academic words, rather than on the highly idiomatic staple words, as is done by Professor Ogden. We do not find the words "can" and "know" in Basic English, but only the words "able" and "knowledge." Instead, therefore, of saying "I do not know," one would have to say "I have no knowledge." "Death" as the less changeable word is chosen instead of "die": consequently in Basic English "Death comes to a man" instead of "he dies." Professor Ogden himself points out that "In Basic we do not *hear* a lark *caroling:* we are *conscious,* however, of the loud, clear song of the bird, with its sweet voice, so full of feeling." Owing to the principle of "higher-level efficiency" and the necessity of choosing words which, by their abstract, general character, could be used for defining others, we find the following typical words: "operation, observation, representative, process, lump, space, vibration, parallel, religion, existence," words which are not found in the other first thousand word lists, such as are made by Thorndike, Knowles, and others.

In consequence of this principle, we find the following curious circumlocutions in *Carl and Anna,* as done into Basic as an illustrative example. "The most fervent image of imagination" becomes "the most burning picture that has existence only in the mind." A "beard" becomes "growth of hair on the face" and a woman's breast becomes a "milk-vessel." The general effect of such a somewhat hard and severe style may be illustrated from the following example:

"Slowly he went to her, feeling her attraction. There was something troubled about her parted lips; at the same time they said 'yes.' He put his arm slowly round her. They were together in one another's arms, not moving. And when, lifting his eyes, he saw her lips open, waiting for him, and *took them again and again,* no word was said."

Pidgin English is a glorious language. It has tremendous possibilities. So far as I know, Bernard Shaw and Otto Jespersen are the only people who have a good word to say for pidgin. In a newspaper interview, Shaw is quoted as saying that the pidgin "no can" is a more expressive and more forceful expression than the "unable" of standard English. When a lady says she is "unable" to come, you have a suspicion she may change her mind and perhaps come after all, but when she replies to your request with an abrupt, clear-cut "no can," you know you have to reckon without her company.

According to the esthetics of Benedetto Croce and his school, any literary or artistic act can be judged only in terms of its expressiveness, irrespective of external standards like meter in poetry or grammar in language. Judged by this Crocean standard, expressions like "no can," "no wanchee," and "maskee," which are always forceful and expressive, have as much literary value as the most polished lines of Milton. Perhaps they gain a little by that comparison. They always express what the speaker means.

Not only does the Italian professor Croce help us to appreciate the literary value of pidgin English, but even the historical dialectic of Karl Marx makes it inevitable that pidgin English shall become the language spoken by all the respectable people of the world in the twenty-fifth century. Advocates of English as an auxiliary international language have often advanced as an argument in its favor the fact that the language is now spoken by over five million people. By this numerical standard, Chinese ought to stand a close second as an international language, since it is spoken by four hundred fifty million, or every fourth human being on earth. The Chinese language has also been considered by philologists like Otto Jespersen and Gabelentz as the simplest, most advanced, and most logical language. In fact, the whole trend of the development of the English language teaches us that it has been steadily advancing toward the Chinese type. English common sense has triumphed over grammatical nonsense and refused to see sex in a tea cup or a writing desk, as modern French and German are still doing. It has practically abolished gender, and it has very nearly abolished case. It has now reached a stage where Chinese was perhaps ten thousand years ago.

Add to this the fact that students of world events always tell us that the future of the world commerce will be around the Pacific, and remember, furthermore, that the future will be a proletarian world, and you have, before your mind, all the historical factors that will make pidgin the inevitable international language five hundred years hence. Even if the population remains what it is today, you will have in the year 2400 A.D. five million people who speak English trading and rubbing shoulders with four hundred fifty million Chinese—all of them with a proletarian temper that dislikes anything so luxurious as English grammar—and you cannot help accepting pidgin English as the only respectable international language of the future.

It is claimed that it was the highly analytic character of the English language, its structural resemblance to Chinese, which enabled Professor Ogden to make a list of eight hundred fifty English words cover a field impossible with a language like French or German. The trouble with Basic English is that it is not analytic enough. We find the word "gramophone," for instance, circumlocuted in Basic English as "a polished black disc with a picture of a dog in front of a horn" (*Carl and Anna,* p. 39). In 2400 A.D., we could call it more simply in real pidgin as "talking box." Basic English is still at a loss to express "telescope" and "microscope." In 2400, we shall call them more simply "look-far-glass" and "show-small-glass." We could dispense with the word "telegraph" (which is not in Basic) and call it "electric report," and replace "telephone" by the pidgin "electric talk." A "cinema" will then simply be "electric picture." And a "radio" will simply be "no-wire-electricity."

There is another way in which the development of pidgin could be used to guide the maker of Basic English in his choice of words. It is an unfortunate fact that Professor Ogden was forced to select words of an abstract, generic character, instead of those of a more specific character. It is a list that smells of the psychological laboratory (with words like "behavior," "reaction," "impulse," "observation," "normal"), unlike pidgin English which grows out of the real workaday life, and which, therefore, includes, by necessity, the words proved by practice to be indispensable. I have heard an old amah swearing "you dam foo" a hundred times to a foreign child in an hour, which shows "you dam foo" is a phrase of very high frequency of use.

One who goes through the list will note that there are no "ladies" and "gentlemen" in Basic, but only "men" and "women," while we know the future Pacific merchant will have to use the words "ladies" and "gentlemen" if he is not to go about referring to every lady as "that woman" and lose his business. Basic English has included the word "able" but not the word "can." Professor Ogden will find, to his sorrow, that in 2400, everybody will be saying the houseboy's "no can" instead of his bookish "able" or "not able."

The man with Basic English could have his "meals," but there will be no "dinner" or "supper." He will look in vain in the Basic menu for steak, cutlet, chop, chicken, or veal. He will order "fowl" and take his chances whether duck, chicken, or game is served, and he will order "fish" and be contented to have salmon or trout as the waiter thinks fit to serve him. If he wants onion, it is suggested that he can ask for "white root that makes eyes full of water." As the word "scramble" is not basic, the nearest expression I can think of for "scrambled egg" is "egg in bad shape," "troubled egg," or "twisted egg" ("disturbed egg" is not Basic). Also for a "poached egg," I can hazard the expression "egg boiled without hard cover in boiling water." And I shall get it.

Any pidgin-speaking boy can draw up a menu to satisfy the average European tourist. He has learned from hard experience that words like "cutlet," "chop," "steak," "fillet," should be included among the first hundred. But in Basic English we cannot find even the already popular *tu-se* ("toast") of modern Chinese. I have drawn up for my own amusement the following Basic menu, which I believe any Cathay Hotel boy could rectify or improve with great effect.

A BASIC MENU

False soup of swimming animal with round hard cover
or
Soup of end of male cow [1]
Fish with suggestion of China or the Peking language
Young cow inside thing nearest the heart boiled in oil [2]
Fowl that has red thing under mouth, that makes funny, hard noise and is eaten by Americans on certain day, [3] *taken with apple cooked with sugar and water, but cold*
Meat with salt preparation that keeps long time
Hot drink makes heart jump or you don't go to sleep

NOTES: [1] We find the word "cow" but not the word "ox" in basic.

[2] This is fried calf's liver. It is not likely to be ambiguous, since the only thing nearest the heart of a calf that the Europeans eat is liver.

[3] In Chinese, "turkey" is simply "fire-hen," from its reputation for eating burning coal.

47

THE DONKEY THAT PAID ITS DEBT

I TOOK a trip to Yangchow, where the idyllic beauty of the "Thin West Lake" made me believe for a time that I was a poet. This differed from the West Lake of Hangchow in that it was no lake at all, but consisted of long, broad, winding waterways that changed their aspect at every corner, thus alternately revealing and concealing their beauties like a Chinese pleasure garden, whereas the West Lake of Hangchow could be surveyed at a glance. It also differed from the West Lake in its greater wildness and seclusion. If the West Lake was like a beautiful woman of thirty in a rich man's home, seeing the Thin West Lake was like meeting with a beautiful maiden in a desert.

Thus seeing the Thin West Lake on a rainy May morning, when the veil of mist hung lightly over it, made one feel that the very air breathed of poetry. One could not think of versifying at such a place: all one had to do to be a poet there was to have a peaceful mind and hold it perfectly focused, as it were, at the highest point of sensibility, and then inhale, instead of expressing, poetry into one's thoughts. Or, one might regard the view before one's eyes as a painting, where there was not a single speck of dust in the air, a single inharmonious line in the picture, or a single trace of human beings to destroy the illusion. The winding waterways, the green shadows of weeping willows, the sweet, silent gurgle of water passing beneath our boat, the low, languorous laughter of the "boat maid," the symphony of birds' songs in the air, the scamper of some startled marsh-inhabiting bird called the *k'u-wa-tsu*—all these in a place filled with dreams of fabulous glory in the bygone centuries, where poets had played and scholars had ruled, combined to make me feel that I was passing one of the most idyllic days of my life.

Imagine, therefore, that against such a background, you were told one of the best humorous tales in the world. This tale of a reincarnated donkey that paid its debt and the memory of the luxurious feeling of being pedicured to high heaven by a Yangchow pedicurist, are two of the best souvenirs I brought back with me from Yangchow. The tale has a humor very much like that of Mark Twain's "Jumping Frog." Like the "Jumping Frog," I believe it must have been a real story, and I shall tell you why one's father can be a real donkey when you have heard the story itself.

There is a hamlet in Anhui called Touniehchen in Chaohsien which is situated on the Chao Lake and connected by a river of about ninety *li* with Wuhu. On account of its geographical importance, Touniehchen is a commercial center for the neighboring four *hsien* of Hofei, Chuanchiao, Chaohsien, and Hanshan. The town has a fairly large population, and its most important trade is rice, besides the import and export of cotton cloth and dry goods.

Some years ago there was an old rice merchant in this town by the name Wang Yungming, who was a good friend of another old rice merchant by the name of Hsieh Fengshan in a neighboring town called Chiungyangchen. They had been friends for years, and during 1931, the year of the great flood, Hsieh was compelled to borrow five hundred dollars from Wang, for which he gave a proper written receipt in Wang's keeping. After the flood, Hsieh then established his business in Hofei on the west, and they saw less of each other. As Wang was well off and they had been good friends, he did not press for the repayment of the loan.

When Hseih Fengshan died, his death reminded Wang of the debt of five hundred dollars which was still due to him. Wang, therefore, started out for Hsieh's home in Chiungyangchen with the I.O.U. in his pocket, ostensibly to attend his friend's funeral, but also to collect the old debt, thus combining business with friendship courtesy.

When Wang entered the Hsieh home, he saw indeed his friend's coffin standing in the hall and the family busy about the usual funeral ceremonies. Hsieh's son came out to receive him with great hospitality and courtesy. This made it somewhat difficult for Wang to broach the topic of the loan, and he thought he would delay a few days until the ceremonies were over.

After a few days, Wang told young Hsieh about the loan,

showing him the I.O.U., and politely asking for its repayment.

"Your father was a great friend of mine," Wang said. "That was why I put off asking him for the repayment. Now that he is dead, I shall be greatly obliged if we can have this settled while I am here."

"Of course, of course, Uncle Wang," said young Hsieh. "You were kind enough to lend us money while we were in trouble, and I must do my best to repay you. If you will kindly wait a few days, I think I shall be able to arrange it."

Wang then went back to his inn, and during the few days that followed, young Hsieh came to see him often. One day Hsieh asked one of his assistants to accompany Wang to a bath in one of the public bathhouses. Wang was now getting impatient to go home, and after the bath he came to Hsieh's home and said he would like to have the money now.

"I have got it ready for you," replied Hsieh. "Now if you will give me the I.O.U., I shall hand over the sum, and all will be settled between us."

Wang then started to get out the receipt. He searched and searched for it in his pocket. It was gone. He was sure he had seen it the night before and had it in his pocket when he went to the bath with Hsieh's assistant, where they had sat side by side.

"Of course, I cannot return you the money unless you produce the I.O.U.," said Hsieh.

Wang was struck dumb with rage and suspicion. Young Hsieh began to say that he had no personal knowledge of the loan, as far as he was concerned, and that obviously one would demand the note back on repayment of a debt.

"Of course, as my father's son," said young Hsieh, "I would honor any debt incurred by my father, signed by his own writing, that is to say, *if* there *was* a debt and *if* there *was* an I.O.U. *at all.*"

Wang was helpless with rage at this insinuation.

"You m-m-m-mean to say . . ." He left it unfinished.

From sly insinuations they came to open altercations.

"Well! Well! Well!" Wang said. "I will not argue with you. Fortunately your father's coffin is still here. We can both swear before your father's coffin."

It was agreed. And Wang swore that if he had not loaned the deceased man money, that if he was here to cheat his son, he was willing to be changed into a donkey in the next incarnation to be ridden by him for life. After the oath, Wang cried bitterly before his friend's coffin. And Hsieh also burned incense and swore that if he was wronging Wang, his deceased father should become a donkey to be ridden by Wang in payment of his debt.

So Wang went back to his inn telling people of the affair of the loan and the oath before the coffin. Then in a rage he left for his home. When he arrived, he told his whole family about it, and they were all enraged.

It happened, then, one rainy afternoon, when Wang was standing with a pipe in front of his house, he saw the old Hsieh enter his door and disappear beyond the parlor. He was delighted and followed him in to have a chat with him, when he suddenly remembered that old Hsieh was dead. He searched through the house, and could not find any trace of him. It must have been old Hsieh's spirit.

While the whole family were held in fear and bewilderment, they heard from the servant that their donkey in the back yard had given birth to a young one. Wang went to the back yard, and, strange to say, the new-born donkey nodded to him, when he saw Wang. And Wang said to the young donkey:

"O young donkey! If you are really Hsieh Fengshan, nod to me three times."

And the young donkey nodded three times. Wang was both amused and puzzled. He fed the young donkey and took good care of him. After a few days, he discovered that under the donkey's belly there was a tuft of hair, resembling the characters *feng* ("phoenix") and *shan* ("hill"), which was old Hsieh's name. The latter character was especially clearly marked. Then Wang was convinced it was his old friend.

The neighborhood then got to know the story, and it spread far and wide in the country, and many people came from a distance to see the strange young donkey that had been born to repay an old debt.

Things were never so strange that they couldn't be stranger still. After a time, Wang rode one day on his donkey and went to Chaohsien to replenish his stock. When he was passing by a certain porcelain shop, the silly donkey went straight into the shop and, without any apparent reason, kicked down a whole shelf of porcelain wares. The shopkeeper demanded payment for the damage, and Wang in his fit of anger struck the donkey and said:

"Shame on you, Hsieh Fengshan!" (For he had always called the donkey by that name.) "Why did you do this and get me into trouble?"

"Why do you call the donkey Hsieh Fengshan?" asked the shopkeeper, puzzled.

Then Wang told him the story of his friend.

"Forget about it, then," said the shop man. "I owed old Hsieh seven dollars. He must have come back to be repaid."

And then they counted the loss, and found it to be slightly over eight dollars, which was accurate enough if interest was added.

The story then grew stranger still and it spread so far that even people in Hsieh's town heard about it. And it came to be talked about that young Hsieh's father had been reincarnated as a donkey, and was being ridden by his old friend Wang. Young Hsieh was so enraged at the story that he prosecuted Wang before the magistrate for fabricating the story to injure his name and make him lose face.

The case, so far as I know, is still pending investigation.

Did Wang really see the spirit of old Hsieh enter his home? How came it that there was a tuft of hair on the donkey's belly, and how exact was that resemblance to old Hsieh's name? As for the story of the porcelain shop, I had heard it personally from a donkey driver on my visit to the Ming Tombs near Peiping in 1922, so that it must have been fastened upon the story, or else, knowing about the old tale, Wang could have arranged with the porcelain shopkeeper to have it happen in the way he wanted. In other words, did Wang viciously fabricate the whole story as a strange form of exacting payment for the five hundred dollars which he knew he could never recover?

What I know is that the whole story is entirely plausible, and Wang got the greatest kick out of it.

48

THE FUTURE OF CHINA

IT IS impossible to discuss the future of China without knowing what we mean by our designation of that vast racial and national entity. And the task is made difficult by the fact that China is swiftly changing, breaking away from its long past, and contains within itself some surprising elements or powers of vitality which do not meet the eye of the person who looks only on the surface.

Even the fortunes of the battlefield and the extent and

eventual outcome of the present Sino-Japanese hostilities cannot be reckoned without a closer knowledge of the emerging Chinese nation that never was a nation, but only a civilization. The future of this belatedly emerging nation will be only superficially affected by the outcome of the war. Personally, I think there is an internal force in China that will bring about a stalemate and virtually win the war. But win or lose, China holds her destiny in her own hands. It is something that nobody else can do anything about, not even Japanese tanks and airplanes.

Since the outbreak of the war, we have had a glimpse of China's new national entity. She has been defeated on the battlefield; she has lost large bits of territory; she has even lost her former capital. But so far nothing has happened to Chinese leadership and the internal solidarity of Chinese resistance. On the other hand, all signs—the reorganization of the Chinese Government, the removal of the capital, the rejection of successive Japanese peace offers, the adoption of the "scorched earth" policy and guerrilla tactics, the intensive training of millions of recruits, and the building of thousands of miles of highway—point to an intensified determination to fight to the end. These things could not have happened five years ago, and they afford a glimpse of that strange force that is transforming China.

It is necessary to go back a little, to twenty-nine years ago. Then, in 1911, the Manchu Empire collapsed. The young republicans thought they could transform this old empire at one stroke into a modern republic. But the republic fell by its own weight into a number of regional "tuchunates," dominated by the surviving "tuchuns," or generals, trained in the Manchu times. Parliamentary government was a failure and was speedily given up, with no defenders.

All this is understandable because, besides the collapse of the empire, there was a collapse of ordinary social and cultural values. Without modern means of communication, unity was a physical impossibility. What happened to Europe after the fall of the empire of Charlemagne or of Napoleon happened in China after the fall of the Manchu Empire. There was a changing balance of power among the old war lords, and a struggle between these and the revolutionary forces.

Eleven years afterward, in 1922, at the Washington conference, the Western powers, undaunted by the temporary chaos in China, affirmed their faith in China's ability to restore order to her own country, and pledged themselves "to give the fullest and most unembarrassed opportunity to China to develop and maintain for herself a stable and effective government."

As a matter of fact, although some Chinese disliked the Washington treaty as insulting, the outward records of China in the preceding ten years did not justify that great faith of the Pacific powers in China's ability "to develop and maintain for herself a stable and effective government." Only far-sighted statesmen were able to see beyond the immediate present, and their faith has been justified by the formation of the Nanking Government, established since 1927, which no one can deny has steadily come up to the expectations of the Western powers as a "stable and effective government," yearly growing in strength and power for internal reconstruction.

The Washington treaty, with its implied belief in the sanctity of the pledged word, gave the Pacific powers a respite in naval armaments and China a real chance to work out her own salvation. Coincident was the fact that during about ten years after the Washington conference, the liberals in Japan were in power and were able to hold back their military dreamers of the Tanaka type. Those ten years following the Washington conference were the only decent years in Japan's relationship with China; the new period began with the Manchurian conquest of 1931.

What really has happened inside China is not the work of any single man, not even Chiang Kai-shek, the most important personal factor in China's developing strength. The force making for an awakened, nationally conscious China is the force of invisible ideas and the circumstances of international contact. Nothing can stop the force of ideas, of newspapers and pictures and magazines, of movies and radios, of increasing roads and means of communication, of increasing public enlightenment.

Men and women became more modern in outlook; a new generation of college professors replaced the old mandarinate (my colleagues in the Peking National University, a Professor of Economics, a Professor of Geology, and a Chancellor who studied education at Columbia, were in the Nanking Cabinet); a new generation of Western-educated bankers and financiers replaced the old financiers of the Peking regime, who were gifted in raising money for the army, not through reform of the monetary system, but through searching out new loopholes in the revenue laws. The younger generation became, if anything, a little bit Leftist and ultra-radical. People who fight over Stalinism and Trotskyism in China can be expected to be socially conscious.

From 1931 on, Japan has performed a signal, invaluable service in intensifying and speeding up this national consciousness. On the government side, schemes for national defense and reconstruction were progressing at amazing speed. Railway lines were pushed rapidly (the Canton-Hankow line was completed by night labor, the workers lighted by torches, in anticipation of Japanese blockades); a network of motor roads grew up throughout the provinces, connecting Nanking with China's southwestern and northwestern provinces; the double-decked steel bridge across the Ch'ientang River at Hangchow and the 7,000,000-Chinese-dollar wharf for ocean liners at Kiangwan were finished just before the hostilities began.

The government's financial position was immensely strengthened by currency reforms, centralization of silver reserve and amalgamation of government banks. College freshmen and secondary school first-year pupils were given military training in camps for three months in many provinces. Evidently China, at long last, had pulled herself together; it was the emergence of a new China which scared Japan. The nationalism that made such internal progress possible is the same nationalism that is determined to resist Japan to the bitter end now. It is not something that can be crushed by an external invasion. Whatever happens, the seed is already there, sure to sprout and come to the light.

Now this new nationalism is under test. That this test came six years after the Mukden incident is to the good of China. As I have said, the Japanese Army has been guilty of aiding and abetting the rise of the nationalist spirit in China, which both logically and actually cannot be distinguished from "anti-Japanism," or hatred of the invader of our home and hearth. During the series of uninterrupted encroachments upon Chinese territory and sovereignty in the six years following the Manchurian conquest (Jehol, Chahar, East Hopei, Suiyuan), awakened national consciousness, synonymous with hatred of the Japanese invaders, has had plenty of time to sink deep into the minds of Chinese of all classes, and it has been intensified by Nanking's suppression of all forms of anti-Japanese expressions or activities through censorship in order to avoid inopportune "incidents."

At this present moment, against her will, Japan is strengthening this very nationalism of China and solidifying Chinese unity. It is clear that Japan has plunged along a road from which there is no retreat. She must go on straight toward the goal of forcing a collapse of Chinese resistance, without hesitation and without regret, although she knows the method employed means raising more and more bitter hatred. If she attains her objective, and China abjectly gives up the battle, well and good; but if she falls short of this objective and there is no collapse of Chinese resistance, she must be prepared to accept the consequences.

I believe Japan is taking very large chances. Anyway, the die is cast, and she knows that henceforth she can have Chinese "co-operation" on the Japan-Manchukuo pattern or not at all. Bombs are bad messengers of love and friendship.

Everywhere a Japanese bomb drops, anti-Japanese hatred sinks into the soul of the Chinese as the metal splinters sink into Chinese bodies. If there was any doubt that Chinese of all classes had heard of Japanese invasions, the airplane trips of Japanese bombers have completely removed it. And when it comes to reaction to alien aggression, the Chinese feel exactly the same as all peoples of other lands. Therefore, I regard the Japanese bombers as the most reliable propaganda arm of Chiang Kai-shek's army, for the Japanese are known to be hard workers.

The obvious conclusion regarding the effect of all this

on the continuance of the war is that Japan will be forced into a prolonged and extremely weakening conflict. Japan's worry will not be how much Chinese territory she can conquer, but how much she can safely hold without great costs and exhausting effects upon her in the face of guerrilla resistance.

In other words, Japan's problem is not how far she can penetrate, but how much Chinese territory she would like to defend for the Chinese puppet regime inside China. For just as Manchukuo requires a permanent station of Japanese troops, so will any puppet regime inside China require permanent occupation by soldiers—and will collapse the moment such forces are withdrawn. The bigger the territory of the puppet regime, the bigger will be the army of occupation required. The application of guerrilla tactics, plus the adoption of the "scorched-earth" policy, which is in itself the surest indication of Chinese determination to fight to the finish, will force a stalemate, which I believe is the only certain outcome.

China's nationalism is under the severest test it can be put to, involving untold sufferings for the people. At the end of the war China will be devastated and Japan will be so weakened that she will become a second-class power. When Japan is forced to call off the invasion by face-saving mediation through a third power, this nationalism will come back to engage in the gigantic task of national rehabilitation. The effects of this war will be felt for a decade in both countries.

Such a China, freed from foreign domination after a terrible ordeal, will, I am quite sure, come back with a new self-confidence and new national pride. But the present struggle means that the work of internal reconstruction which began some eight years ago will have to begin again from a lower level than before. It means that Chiang Kai-shek will become a national hero and that the people now willingly co-operating with the present government will be infused with a new loyalty. It means also a new respect for the soldier, whom the Chinese had always held in contempt, and a new general interest in the forces of national defense.

What has happened is going to continue to happen; the unseen force of modern ideas will take hold of this old, cultured people. For no modern people, with the intelligence and industry which the Chinese have, can ever be conquered. Bismarck smashed France, Bismarck thought, and the Allies smashed Germany, the Allies thought. Japan is going to smash this new nationalism in China (which is the purpose of this war), so Japan is thinking now. If Russia comes in at the end of the conflict to deal a smashing blow to Japan at the point of the latter's near-exhaustion, Russia will think she is going to smash Japan for ever, but can a modern Japanese nation be smashed? There are things that force cannot smash.

If, therefore, nationalism in China is already a fact, China, I believe, will stage a comeback during the aftermath of this war, helped by the lesson of the war and by her own enormous vitality. I believe the nation will be electrified by this experience and will set to work with a will on measures of internal reconstruction. The most valuable gift of the war is, I believe, the lesson of discipline, which is usually not the outstanding virtue of the Chinese. Mme. Chiang will go on with her New Life Movement, which will receive through this lesson a new meaning.

We shall, therefore, have a regime characterized in several ways. First, Chiang's prestige will be immeasurably increased, and that will greatly facilitate his work. Second, the people will be more war-conscious and more militaristic, certainly more nationalistic. Third, the people will certainly become more socially conscious, especially through political indoctrination during their training for guerrilla warfare, and rural reforms and rehabilitation will occupy the foremost place in the leaders' minds. Fourth, a good number of the present civil leaders will be weeded out.

The check to communism in China lies in the inherent Chinese tradition, while the check to fascism will lie in the same tradition and in Chiang's gaining stature as a leader with a broadening outlook. The road for China will remain the road of democracy.

The Chinese love of moderation is important. China is not Japan, and never will be. Sooner or later, after this war, the privileges of extraterritoriality for Westerners in China will have to be given up and foreign concessions returned. But I do not believe the change will be characterized by violence. An important factor in the situation is that China will be in dire need of foreign capital for rehabilitation, and the democratic powers will certainly use the need as a lever to keep their position as long as possible. But China's international relationships will be characterized by a new and more healthful atmosphere of mutual respect.

As for Japan, the path of Sino-Japanese relationships will be strewn with newer and greater problems, but it will be as much Japan's job as China's to tackle them, and I am inclined to think Japan will be too busy thinking about her own economic problems to tackle China's.

As for China's ever coming to a really amicable relationship with Japan after the war, the Japanese have destroyed all chance of that. Whether as conquerors or neighbors, they lack the political genius for winning people. "Manchukuo" tells the whole story. The Japanese are and always will remain poor colonists.

49

THE REAL THREAT: NOT BOMBS, BUT IDEAS

IN THE progress of human civilization the arts of living and the arts of killing—artcraft and warcraft—have always existed side by side. No history of any nation shows that a period of peace without domestic or foreign wars ever existed for more than 300 years. This seems to derive from the fact that man is both a fighting and a peaceful animal. In him the fighting instinct and the instinct for peaceful living—which I call the carnivorous and the herbivorous instincts—are strangely mixed.

This is not to imply a state of human imperfection; it may be questioned whether the kind of civilization wherein man is so thoroughly tamed and domesticated that there is no more fight left in him would be worth having at all. Life is, or should be, accompanied by struggle, or else the racial fiber degenerates, which happens within the amazingly short period of a few generations as in a well-provided family.

I am not trying to condone war, but am merely pointing out our biological heritage. In the world of nature the warring instinct and the instinct to live are different aspects of the same thing. Those primeval biological instincts go deeper than any temporary ideologies or political creeds. In the biological world merciless wars have always existed side by side with the most persistent displays of love for the young and all those manifestations of courtship which produce beauty and which we know as the charm and fragrance of the flower, the caroling of the lark, and the song of the cricket.

If it is somewhat disheartening to the student of nature that the most ruthless war is going on above ground and underground day and night in what is apparently a peaceful forest, or to reflect that the kingfisher sitting on a branch so peacefully in a sunset has just returned from murder of an innocent minnow, it is also a source of comfort to know that nature's instinct to live is always overpowering and manages to stage a most impressive comeback after a natural disaster. Anybody who visited the coasts of Long Island Sound and saw the green trees and peaceful landscape after the disastrous hurricane of the autumn before, cannot help being impressed by nature's persistent urge to live.

Today, once more, Europe is ravaged by war. To every observer war seemed inevitable after Munich, because peace was so much like war that, to the average Frenchman or Englishman, a temporary peace seemed infinitely more devastating. To add to the confusion the fighting man still parades as a lover of peace, and aggressors accuse their victims as "warmongers." Hitler, returning red-handed from

the murder of Poland, offered that same "outstretched hand"
to Europe and asked innocently, "Why should there be
war?" And Japan, plunging into a continental slaughter,
claims only the desire to set up a "new order." Peace and
war are worse confounded than ever.

What is the meaning of all this? Has man's instinct for
peaceful living been temporarily inhibited, overshadowed,
and perhaps destroyed by the warring instinct? And will
civilization—meaning the arts, the religions, the common
faiths of mankind, the modern conquests of science, and the
arts of living—will this modern civilization be destroyed?
Let us take up the second proposition first.

Many people are horrified by the thought of great cities
demolished by air bombing, and many foremost thinkers
of today are rather inclined to believe that modern civilization as we know it will be destroyed. I beg profoundly to
differ.

Knowing that the warring instinct is but another aspect
of the instinct for living, and believing that no man going to
battle has ever renounced the desire to live, I think the
instinct for living is the stronger of the two and hence
cannot be destroyed. Since that instinct cannot be destroyed,
civilization, too, or the arts of living, cannot be destroyed.
What do we mean when we say that by this war modern
civilization will be destroyed?

Physically the arts and sciences may receive a temporary
setback, but I wager that after the war hens will still lay
eggs and men will still not have forgotten how to make
omelettes. Sheep will still grow wool and English mills will
still turn out tweeds and homespuns. The physical fea-
tures of a city may be altered under the most ruthless bombing, and conceivably some old manuscripts or even the

Magna Carta, in the British Museum, may be lost or go up in flames. Some English poets and French scientists may have been killed by shrapnel and some valuable laboratory equipment, or even all of Oxford, may be wiped out. Still, the underground Bodleian Library cannot be destroyed. Still, the scientific method will survive; it is inconceivable that all treatises and textbooks of science will disappear. Gramophone records and Chopin's music will still be there, because the love for music will still be there.

The quality of manhood may suffer perceptibly from the slaughter of the flower of the nation. But so long as a nation is not completely annihilated with the worst aerial bombings, modern civilization and all the heritage of the arts and the sciences will be carried on. After war and destruction the generous instinct for peaceful living, the creative forces of human ingenuity will restore Europe in an amazingly short period.

The lesson seems plain that mere physical violence never accomplishes anything. China provides a good example. The destruction of Chinese schools, universities, and cultural institutions by the Japanese in the present war could never be more systematic, more thorough and more physically complete. Yet it would be far-fetched to say that modern Chinese culture is thereby destroyed. The professors and students of a university in Chekiang marched a thousand miles overland from the southeast and reopened their classes in Southwest Yunnan.

Nothing is lost if man is not lost. Devotees of China's ancient culture may express an exquisite regret that the world's only extant imperial library of Yunglo was burned during the sack of Peking by English and French troops in 1859. But what of it for the Chinese nation as a whole? The most ruthless destruction of Confucian books and persecution of Confucianists under the dictator Ch'in Shih-hwang (builder of the Great Wall) failed to destroy the Confucian culture.

This leads to the subtler, nonphysical aspects of the question and the positive side of human living. Modern civilization would be destroyed if the things that make for civilization, the things we take for granted—freedom of belief, the rights and liberties of the individual, democracy, and that now tottering faith in the common man—if these things were destroyed. Without war, a totalitarian State which deprives men of these gifts of civilization and sets men as spies upon their fellow men has already begun to destroy civilization. With a nation not so easily regimented, where the spirit of man still remains free, that civilization cannot be destroyed by a war.

It is, in fact, entirely possible for civilization to destroy itself by subordinating the instinct for peaceful living to the other instinct for killing. Civilization can be destroyed unless these simple values of human life are more jealously guarded and the simple liberties and privileges of living are more consciously appreciated. There is every sign of the danger that in contemporary thinking and contemporary life such common privileges of living are increasingly giving way to the claims of the State-monster. The citizen of a totalitarian State in Europe has already lost certain privileges and liberties of thinking and living which the savages of Africa have always enjoyed and are still enjoying.

In fact, we have already traveled a long way from civilization as ordinarily understood. All nature loafs. Then civilization came, offering man certain comforts of living in exchange for certain restrictions of liberty, generally called a sense of duty. No horse has a sense of duty, and every car-rier-pigeon flies home just because he likes it. But man was put to work.

First, he was told to work for a living. Next he was told to war for a living in defense of his right to work. And now we are told to put guns before butter and regard it as a nobler form of death to die with one's army boots on than with one's boots off in bed. We are going back to nature without the natural liberties of nature. Man has ration cards and a sense of duty. A million automatons, completely trained and regimented to think in one direction, either curse or praise the Soviet Union as their master tells them to do.

And so what threatens civilization today is not war itself or the destruction of war but the changing conceptions of life values entailed by certain types of political doctrines. These doctrines directly impinge upon man's ordinary, na-tural privileges of living and subordinate them to the needs of national killing. The importance of killing supersedes the importance of living, from the totalitarian standpoint.

It cannot be denied that from the point of view of the State, organized for war and conquest, totalitarianism has everything to be said for it, but from the standpoint of the individual as the ultimate aim served by civilization, and for the purpose of enjoying the ordinary blessings of living, it has nothing to be said on its side. It is neither the machine nor war that is destroying modern civilization but the tend-ency to surrender the rights of the individual to the State which is such a powerful factor in contemporary thinking.

The Roman Empire was probably destroyed by rats or by mosquitoes and ultimately by a deterioration in manhood. Modern civilization can possibly be destroyed by the kind of peace that causes a similar racial deterioration, either in the physical sense, as Professor Hooton suggests, or in the spiritual sense of loss of ordinary human liberties. Physically the twentieth-century man wearing a gas-mask snout is horrifying enough to frighten a caveman; spiritually, in certain countries, I doubt that he is more respectable to look at.

The contempt for the common man has gone far enough. In a totalitarian world Whitman's "Song of the Open Road" will read like a forgotten dream.

> Afoot and light-hearted I take to the
>   open road,
> Healthy, free, the world before me,
> The long brown path before me leading
>   wherever I choose.

And his warning will not be lost:

> O highway I travel, do you say to me,
>   *Do not leave me?*
> Do you say, *Venture not—if you leave
>   me you are lost?*

Only by recapturing that dream of human freedom and restoring the value and importance of the common man's rights and liberties of living can that undermining threat to modern civilization be averted. More than ever I believe that the Great Vagabond who proudly refuses to give up an inch of his liberties will be the savior of the world.

I started out by saying that the warring instinct and the instinct for peaceful living are different aspects of the same thing. It is seldom realized that the volunteer who enlists to go to the front is as much following an instinct for new venture upon the open road as the more noble desire to seek death at the cannon's mouth.

It is not a true picture of war at the front to say that the soldier is more excited by the capture of an enemy than by the capture of a stray chicken for the evening meal. The exact reverse is true. Out there on the open road one suddenly realizes that the gift of life is all the more precious, that life is all the sweeter in the presence of death. Out in the trenches people do not brood over their enemies until they get up enough hatred to go out and kill the enemy.

An amateur poet reads his newly inspired limerick at the expense of the field rat or the village maiden; a corporal smokes his pipe and says not a word, while the company listens to the reading of an old novel, perhaps of Bulwer-Lytton, by a comrade; a white-faced, sensitive young man of eighteen comes in with his amazing discovery of violets in the neighboring battered village; someone takes a guitar and sings. At the front the caroling of the lark in the sky and the song of the cricket underground seem more enchanting, more appreciated.

All of a sudden the soldier sees the great naked truth that life is worth living for its own sake. As he looks back upon the people living in the rear, silly common aspects of ordinary living assume an exaggerated importance and a strange fascination. In the first flush of war excitement a volunteer may jump into his khaki shirt and uniform with glee, but after two or three years in the trenches, wearing a red tie and walking with one's sweetheart leisurely of a Sunday afternoon seem to be the only things worth living for. The importance of wearing a red tie is fully appreciated when you cannot wear it. To the soldier returning on leave the most common sights of city or country life—a hot-dog stand, the neon lights at night, even the traffic lights—seem good and reassuring. Even being a lazy louse lying in bed without the hallucination of the reveille seems to constitute an august virtue and a permanent achievement of human civilization.

In fact, one suddenly realizes that all the good things of life—the morning coffee, fresh air, a stroll in the afternoon, even dashing for the subway or dodging friends among commuters in the morning train—constitute civilization because they constitute the very end of living. War makes us realize the importance of the things we ordinarily take for granted. No one values a luxurious shave in a barber shop more than a soldier returning from the front.

That the end of living is just living itself is so obvious that we never thought of it, and in times of peace we even question it. Moralists, for example, seem to despise the act of lying in bed, and theologians used to think that to be uncomfortable was to be virtuous. But in the soldier at the front the conviction must sooner or later grow that lying in bed is one of the supreme gifts of civilization and that to sleep with one's boots off is an incomparably truer form of living than sleeping with one's boots on.